Sequential Movements

ADVANCED LABANOTATION SERIES

EDITOR
Ann Hutchinson Guest
Director, Language of Dance® Centre, London, UK

Vol. 1, 1:
Canon Forms
by Ann Hutchinson Guest
and Rob van Haarst

Vol. 1, 2:
Shape, Design, Trace Patterns
by Ann Hutchinson Guest
and Rob van Haarst

Vol. 1, 3:
Kneeling, Sitting, Lying
by Ann Hutchinson Guest
and Rob van Haarst

Issue 4:
Sequential Movements
by Ann Hutchinson Guest
and Joukje Kolff

Issue 5:
Hands, Fingers
by Ann Hutchinson Guest
and Joukje Kolff

Issue 6:
Floorwork, Basic Acrobatics
by Ann Hutchinson Guest
and Joukje Kolff

Issue 7:
Center of Weight
by Ann Hutchinson Guest
and Joukje Kolff

Issue 8:
Handling of Objects, Props
by Ann Hutchinson Guest
and Joukje Kolff

Issue 9:
Spatial Variations
by Ann Hutchinson Guest,
and Joukje Kolff

Sequential Movements

BY

ANN HUTCHINSON GUEST

AND

JOUKJE KOLFF

DANCE
BOOKS

©2003 Ann Hutchinson Guest. All rights reserved

Dance Books Ltd,
4 Lenten Street, Alton, Hampshire GU34 1HG

Printed in the United Kingdom by H. Charlesworth & Co.,
Huddersfield

ISBN: 1 85273 098 6

This book was written and produced at the Language of Dance® Centre:
    The Language of Dance® Centre
    17 Holland Park
    London W11 3TD
    United Kingdom
    T: +44 (0)20 7229 3780
    F: +44 (0)20 7792 1794
    web: http://www.lodc.org
    e-mail: info@lodc.org

Ann Hutchinson Guest

Joukje Kolff

Contents

Introduction to the Series   xi

Preface   xiii

Acknowledgements   xv

1   Analysis of Sequential Movements   2
     Outward Sequential Movement
     Outward Succession   4
     Inward Sequential Movement
     Inward Succession

2   Method of Writing Sequential Movement   6
     Without Change of Direction
     With Change of Direction

3   Sequential Movements for Leg Gestures   8
     Forward Sequential Leg Gestures
     Backward Sequential Leg Gesutres

4   Performance of Successions for Arm Gestures   10
     Direction of Displacement
     Appearance, Subsidence   12

5   Surface Leading in Successions   14
     Surface Guiding
     Timing of Guidance

6   Overlapping Sequences, Successions   16
     Sequences not Overlapping
     Overlapping Sequences
     Without Change of Direction

7   Sequential Rotations   18
    Sequential Rotations, Twists in the Arm
    Sequential Twists of the Torso
    Sequential Pivot Turns

8   Arm Successions with Rotations   20
    Rotations within the Arm
    Successions with Upper Arm Rotation

9   Successions, Ripples in the Hand   22
    Direction of Displacement
    Surface Leading   23

10 Partial Sequence in the Arm   24
    Ending Part for a Sequence or Succession
    Origin of an Outward Sequential Movement, Succession

11 Central Sequential Movements   26

12 Sequential Movements for the Torso   28
    Sequential Torso Movements on the Floor
    Sequential Torso Movements while Standing

13 Successions in the Torso   30
    Outward Succession
    Degree of Displacement

14 Sequential Movements for Contracting, Folding   32

15 Body Waves   34
    Direction of a Body Wave
    Standard Description of a Forward Body Wave   35
    Body Waves in Different Directions   36
    Waves Stressing More Than One Direction
    One-Sided Emphasis
    Indicating Body Wave Action   38

Contents

Sequential Actions Added

16 Impulse in the Body   40

17 Examples of Inward Sequential Movements   42

18 Reading Examples   46
    Body Waves with Accompanying Arm Movements
    Humphrey Sideward Sequential Movements   48
    Humprey Sagittal Sequential Movement
    'Falls'   50
    Backward Fall and Recovery from Humprey's First Series of Fall
    Hand Ripples   52
    Partial Sequential Movements for the Arm   54
    Central Sequential Movements for the Arm
    Sequential Movement of the Leg
    Torso Succession   58
    Body Waves

Appendix: Historical Background on Labanotation Textbooks   62

Notes   65

Bibliography   70

Index   71

Useful Contact Information   79

Introduction to the Series

The <u>Advanced Labanotation</u> series provides a detailed exposition of the many topics introduced in the chapters of the 1970 textbook *Labanotation - The System of Analyzing and Recording Movement*. To make the material immediately accessible to the reader, each book in this series begins at a basic level, thus avoiding the need for immediate reference to other texts.

Within the series each topic is published independently as soon as it is completed in order to make the information immediately available. Topics for which there is at present a lack of information available, and those for which there is an immediate need, are being presented first.

Detailed theoretical exposition is supported by appropriate notated examples, and, where needed, figure illustrations of the movements and positions. A selection of reading materials from choreographic scores illustrates the different points, with the examples taken from various sources and styles of movement. Finally, a detailed index facilitates rapid access to required information and, for the researcher, meticulous endnotes and a bibliography indicate background and sources.

Preface

A sequential movement, a succession, is one in which movement flows from one part of the body to another in succession, passing from joint to joint, or from vertebra to vertebra in the case of successions in the spine.

When a change of direction occurs for a limb or for the torso, a sequential flow alters the manner of performance. Instead of the limb as a whole moving to and arriving at the new direction, one part of the limb after another moves to and arrives at the new direction. In this investigation the term *sequential* is used as a general term and is specifically applied to directional changes, performed in such a manner.

When there is no change of direction for a limb or the spine, a sequential flow is usually called a *succession*. The term *undulation* is also appropriate. A small succession, often performed rather rapidly, is called a *ripple*. Such successions and ripples are familiar, for example, in Asian Pacific dance.

Movement of this kind which passes through the whole body is called a *body wave*.

Twists (rotations) in the limbs may occur sequentially, i.e. as a succession, as may pivot turns.

The exact size of displacement for sequential movements and successions will vary somewhat from one performer to another, as will the degree of involvement of the upper body and initiation from the center when such occur.

As with many other topics, personal demonstration is often needed to make the understood performance differences clear. Many forms of dance training or other movement training do not involve this kind of movement, thus this exploration may be unfamiliar and some personal instruction may need to be sought.

Acknowledgements

Analysis of sequential movements, successions, and body waves were especially featured in the Jooss-Leeder modern dance technique and were of particular interest to Sigurd Leeder who contributed the signs for these movements. Body waves were also a distinctive part of the technique taught by Ted Shawn.

We are grateful to Charles Woodford, Karoun Tootikian, and Marcia Heard for permission to reproduce appropriate excerpts from scores.

For checking the drafts of this material and for actively taking part in discussions concerning issues and problems we gratefully acknowledge the help of our consultants, Jacqueline Challet-Haas, Ilene Fox, Janos Fügedi, David Henshaw, Sheila Marion, and Lucy Venable whose detailed and judicious comments contributed much to the correction and clarification of working drafts.

Our thanks go to Jane Dulieu for proof-reading with her keen eye for accuracy and to Roma Dispirito for her contribution to producing the Labanotation on *Calaban*.

The research for this issue of Advanced Labanotation and its production have been made possible through funding from the National Endowment for the Humanities, the Arts and Humanities Research Board and the John Simon Guggenheim Memorial Foundation. We are grateful for their generous support.

We are also indebted to Andy Adamson who developed the *Calaban* software used to produce the Labanotation graphics and specifically to Warwick Hampden-Woodfall for his technical support in guiding us through the vagaries and moods of our computer equipment.

Sequential Movements

1 Analysis of Sequential Movement

1.1.   Sequential movements occur in two settings: a) as a manner of performing a directional change for a limb or the spine; b) as an action within the limb or spine without change of direction. In this book the term succession is generally used for the latter.

1.2.   A sequential movement was originally written as a series of parts leading, as in **1a**.[1] Although this description produces a somewhat similar result, it places focus on the individual body parts and not on the successive flow of the action through the limb. Because **1a** begins with indication of shoulder leading, it gives too marked a shoulder involvement at the start. The flow should originate at the base of the arm in the shoulder muscles without displacing the shoulder, it then travels out through each subsequent joint in turn.

1.3.   An action similar to an outward flow could be written as in **1b**, passing through elbow folding and then wrist folding as the arm is raised. This notation, which is not necessarily the equivalent of **1a**, features the actions of elbow and wrist joints and the degree of overlap, specifics not required in an ordinary sequential movement/succession. Note that thumb facing has been added here to clarify palm facing for the end of the movement.

1.4.   Neither of the notations of 1a or 1b gives the essential idea and intention of a sequential movement, a succession. The specific signs used are presented on page 7. But first, analysis of the movements is needed for clarification. Two basic forms of sequential flow/succession exist: outward and inward.

1.5.   **Outward Sequential Movement.** When a sequential movement occurs with a change in direction, one part of the limb after the other moves into the new direction indicated. For an outward succession this action can be compared to laying a scarf on the floor, **1c**. In this example the part nearest the floor (the base, here pinned to the floor to make clear which is the free end) will reach the floor first and each succeeding part will in turn become horizontal.

1.6.   An unemphasized outward sequence occurs when a person lies down in a comfortable manner from a sitting position. The sequence takes place in the spine, **1d**, from the base of the spine headwards (see Section 12 for sequential spatial changes of the torso).

Analysis of Sequential Movement

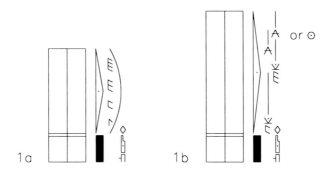

Outward Sequential Movement

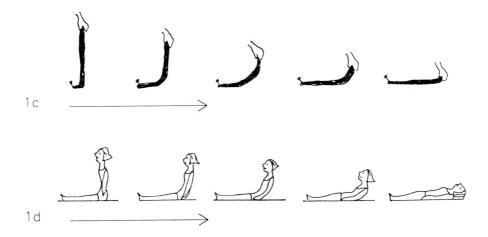

1.7.   **Outward Succession.** When a succession occurs, the limb as a whole retains its previous direction. A very slight displacement must occur to allow the succession to form and progress. If the limb is extended, there must be a slight drawing in to provide 'slack,' just as a caterpillar draws in its rear end (its 'base') in order to progress forward through this succession (undulation) in the body, **1e**.[2] Note: when there is no other indication of change, the limb finishes in the position and state in which it started, e.g. if the limb is extended at the start, it will finish extended; if bent it will finish bent (see **2e** and **2f**).

1.8.   **Inward Sequential Movement.** In an inward sequence the movement commences at the extremity and flows toward the center, i.e. the base. The extremity is the first part to take the new direction and each neighboring part follows until finally the base of the limb takes the new direction. The illustration of **1f**. shows a scarf being sequentially lifted off the ground.

1.9.   An inward sequence occurs when a performer sits up from a lying position; the sequence takes place in the spine, the head being the first to move, **1g**. When the head arrives at the vertical it remains in that direction, it is not carried further as the rest of the torso comes up (see Section 12 for sequential changes of the torso).

1.10.   **Inward Succession.** The limb as a whole retains its previous direction, the ripple starts at the extremity and moves inward. For a caterpillar this means starting at the head, **1h**.

Outward Succession

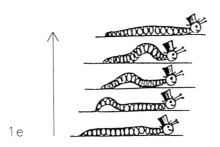

1e

Inward Sequential Movement

1f

1g

Inward Succession

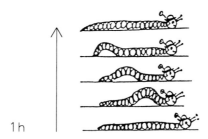

1h

2 Method of Writing Sequential Movement

2.1.   Because the essence of such sequential movements and successions is *the flow* going through the body part, a special sign was introduced to focus on this aspect.[3] For this particular manner of performing a movement, the specific symbols of **2a** and **2b** are provided.[4] These are not to be confused with the increase and decrease signs of **2c** and **2d**, which are also used for toward and away. It was established that for clear identification the sequential/succession signs should occupy only one square, i.e. the same length as the width of the column.[5]

2.2.   **Without Change of Direction.** The sign of **2a** states an outward sequence moving from the base of the body part involved to the extremity. When there is no change of direction the succession sign is followed by a duration line to indicate timing as in **2e**. It is important to note that the timing for a single succession includes the 'subsidence', the return to the normal state or situation. Such a succession can occur for a limb that is already flexed; in **2f** a succession will occur without basically changing the situation of the arm, after the necessary slight displacement it will return to its previous state.

2.3.   **With Change of Direction.** The sign of **2a** is placed as a presign before the appropriate direction symbol when the timing of the sequential movement and the change of direction are the same, as in **2g**. When placed within a curved vertical 'passing state' bow, the timing of the sequential action is shown by the length of the bow. In **2h** the timing of the sequential action is shown to be the same as the change of direction (see Section 4.5 - 4.7 for appearance and subsidence).

2.4.   If the sequential activity is of a shorter duration, as in **2i**, the bow is shortened; here the sequential action occurs only during the first half of the movement, thus the succession will probably be completed by the time the arm reaches the diagonal direction on its way to the side. Ex. **2j** is a more precise statement for this event.

2.5.   One sequential movement can occur over two directions. In **2k** the sequential movement starts as the arm moves toward forward middle; the arm does not arrive at normal extension in that direction but continues to the sideward destination. By the time it arrives the sequential flow has concluded.

Basic Signs for Sequential Movement

2a ⋁   2b ⋀

2c ⋁   2d ⋀

Without Change of Direction

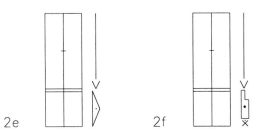

2e   2f

With Change of Direction

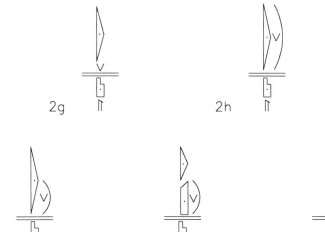

2g   2h

2i   2j   2k

3 Sequential Movements for Leg Gestures

3.1.   **Forward Sequential Leg Gestures.** The focus of sequential movements and successions is usually on the arms and spine, these being more flexible in their range of movement than the legs. There are, however, certain familiar usages that occur in leg gestures where the limb 'unfolds' with an outward sequence.[6] A typical example is **3a**, the forward movement starting in the thigh rather than the whole leg moving forward in one piece. As mentioned before, to achieve this successive action the leg must bend slightly at the start; this is not written.

3.2.   Such 'soft' leg gestures often occur in classical ballet, as in **3b** where it is often used as a preparation for a step into *arabesque*, **3c**. Despite the outward rotation of the legs, the movement starts in the thigh, the movement being led by the inner surface of the thigh, then the inner surface of the lower leg and on through the foot. This graceful movement is different from **3d** in which the leg extends forward from a low *retiré* position resulting in a more 'placed', academic version, the foot moving forward on a straight line. An 'unfolding' may also occur after a *retiré* position, as in **3e** in which the unfolding takes an 'over the top' curve.

3.3.   **Backward Sequential Leg Gestures.** A backward sequential action for the leg would seem possible, certainly in the intention of the performer, but in fact it poses a problem because, theoretically, it is not a correct description of what is desired. The notation of **3f** is sometimes met and is intended to be the backward equivalent action of the forward movement of **3e**. Because of the structure of the hip and leg this outward sequence is not physically possible; to extend the leg backward the foot and lower leg must precede the thigh thus it cannot be an outward sequential flow. The same problem exists for **3g**. A more accurate indication would be to write an inward succession, as in **3h,** or to show the foot leading the action, **3i**. Neither of these is what performers have in mind; they want the feeling of **3a** or **3b** applied to the backward direction. Thus, the use of **3f** for **3g** is an understandable convention.

Forward Sequential Leg Gestures

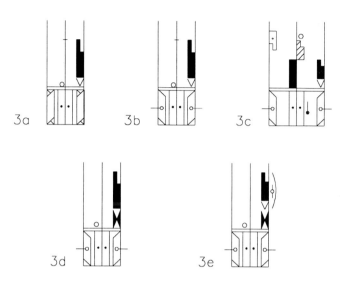

Backward Sequential Leg Gestures

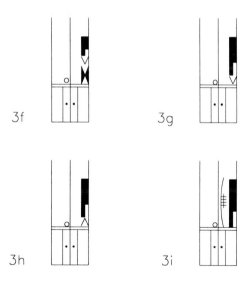

4 Performance of Successions for Arm Gestures

4.1.   **Direction of Displacement.** A simple outward sequential movement, as in **4a**, or a succession, as in **4b** is performed as follows: the initiation comes from the shoulder muscles without any displacement of the shoulder joint, the 'wave' then flows through the upper arm, elbow, lower arm, wrist and hand, dissipating as it reaches the extremity, the finger tips. In a succession such as **4b**, as each part is passed through, it returns to its normal state. At the end the whole limb is in its previous state and alignment.

4.2.   The manner of performing a succession, an undulation, can be varied by the direction in which the slight displacement occurs, or the difference may be caused by which surface of the limb, or change of surfaces, guides the succession. (This latter will be dealt with in the next section.)

4.3.   The method of writing a displacement into a specific direction is to place the appropriate pin within the curved vertical bow, **4c**.[7] This displacement is temporary and will disappear. A downward succession is shown in **4d**. During one succession two displacements can occur. In **4e** the limb displaces upward, then downward before returning to its normal placement.

4.4.   The rotational state of the arm and the direction of the displacement will result in a particular surface of the limb being temporarily involved. In **4f** the outward rotation followed by the upward sequential displacement results in the inner surface of the arm being used without being designated or emphasized. In a similar way the inward rotation in **4g** and the backward displacement will cause the inner surface to be involved, but without its being specified. The degree of rotation will affect which surface is used.

Direction of Displacement

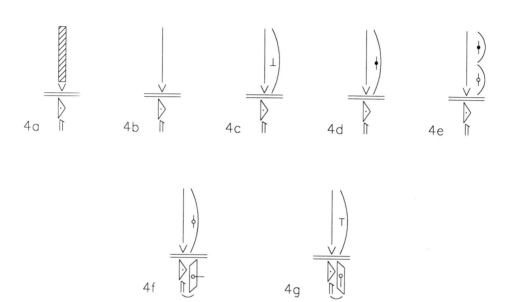

4.5.   **Appearance, Subsidence.** For a movement involving a directional change, a sequential action begins at the start and is completed at the end when the limb arrives at its destination. In the case of a succession through the limb when there is no spatial change in location, the wave appears at the start and, as it travels through the limb, the minor displacement subsides, the subsidence concluding at the end of the action.

4.6.   Ex. **4h** begins with the arm sideward, palm down; no direction of displacement for the succession is given, it is left open. In **4i** an upward deviation (displacement) is stated. What should happen in **4i** is clarified in the diagram of **4j**. The curved bow of 'a' indicates the appearance of the upward displacement, that of 'b' the subsidence. These should be spread harmoniously throughout the action.

4.7.   This involvement of part after part is spelled out in **4k**. For our purpose here, the shoulder joint is stated as being specifically involved at the start which would not usually occur. The inverted V cancellation sign has the meaning of 'disappear'. Should the upward deviation occur only near the beginning, as in **4l**, the subsidence will take longer, the action of the lower parts of the arm will be less, they will not have spatial displacement while the succession flows through them. A pictorial rendition might look like **4m**, though such successions do not lend themselves to graphic representation.

Appearance, Subsidence

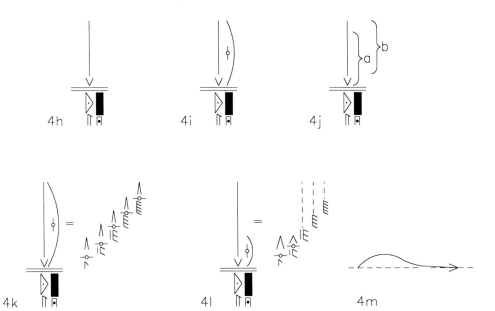

5 Surface Leading in Successions

5.1.   The following examples feature the arm in a sideward direction, a placement frequently used in some forms of Asian Pacific dance where arm successions (ripples) are a salient part of the dance. As with other successions, to provide this articulation, the arm will need to flex slightly. As mentioned before, this slight flexion (which is not indicated here) has disappeared by the end of the movement. The following exploration involves use of the surfaces and edges of the arm to guide the limb articulations.[8]

5.2.   **Surface Guiding.** The starting position for the arm in **5a**, followed by an upward succession, suggests that it will be guided by the outer surface of the arm, a familiar direction for this arm placement. In **5b** guiding with the outer surface is specifically stated. With the palm facing forward in **5c**, the thumb-edge guidance will probably be in the upward direction; in **5d** the deviation is specified.

5.3.   **Timing of Guidance.** Guiding with a surface really only occurs during the first half of the movement; the subsequent 'subsiding', the return to alignment can not be with the same guidance as in **5e** in which the recovery (the subsidence) is without a guidance. Because the vertical bow ends before the succession, the guidance ends sooner and the limb returns to its previous alignment.

5.4.   In **5f** the thumb-edge guidance for the forward displacement causes an initial inward arm rotation. This guidance ends half way through, thus the rotation disappears and the 'subsidence' occurs with the thumb-edge again facing up, **5g**. It should be noted that the bow for deviation is drawn for the full length of the movement because the deviation does not peter out until the end of the bow. In **5h** the upward deviation has no guidance at the start but the subsidence is led by the inner arm.

5.5.   **Surface Leading during Appearance and Subsidence.** In **5i** two guidances are specified within one succession. The initial rising is guided by the thumb-edge, whereas the subsidence, the return to alignment, is guided by the little finger-edge. Statement of such guidances gives them importance, there will be a slight presence of energy, of emphasis for the little finger-edge during the downward movement, i.e. the return to alignment. Ex. **5j** is the reverse, a downward deviation guided first by the little finger-edge, then by the thumb-edge during the return to alignment.

5.6.   The double deviation as well as a double part leading in **5k** provides a combination of **5e** and **5f**. For this and all these examples it must be clear in the performance that only one succession occurs.

Surface Guiding

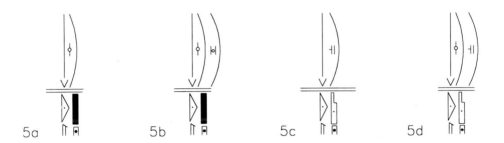

Timing of Guidance

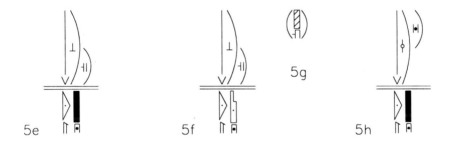

Surface Leading during Appearance and Subsidence

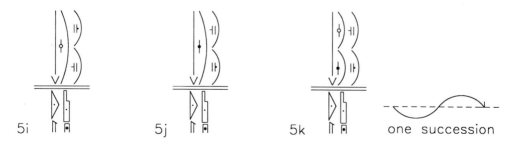

6 Overlapping Sequences, Successions

6.1.   **Sequences Not Overlapping.** Each of the symbols **2a** and **2b** (repeated here) represents one complete sequential movement or succession. It is quite common, whether moving to another direction or remaining in the same location, for a new succession to start before the previous one is finished. We give first examples of this with change of direction for the arm. In **6a** the whole arm moves up to the side and then down again in the normal manner. In **6b** the arm is lifted sequentially, arriving at the normal sideward middle situation; it then immediately lowers sequentially, a separate activity.

6.2.   **Overlapping Sequences.** It is possible for the downward sequence to start before the sideward sequence has concluded, **6c**. Normally, the arm could not move into two different directions at the same time, but, because of the sequential action, it is possible and not so unusual (imagine exaggerated 'flapping one's wings' sequentially).

6.3.   Placement in the adjacent column for the symbols for the downward sequence is generally understood to refer to the arm without addition of a specific indication. However, should there be doubt, use can be made of the device of the small horizontal staple at the start to signify that the adjacent column is also for the arm, **6d**.

6.4.   **Without Change of Directions.** Without the arm changing direction overlapping successions may also occur, as in **6e** which shows a second ripple starting before the first is concluded. The directions for the displacements are given in **6f**. Note that it is usual in such overlapping successions for the second one to be in the opposite direction to the first.

Sequences Not Overlapping

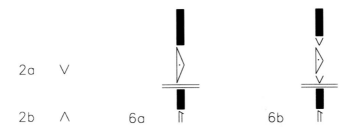

2a ∨   6a

2b ∧   6b

Overlapping Sequences

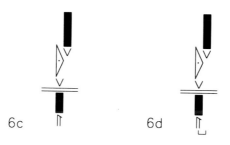

6c   6d

Without Change of Direction

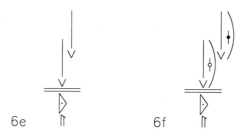

6e   6f

7 Sequential Rotations

7.1.   **Sequential Rotations, Twists in the Arm.** In **7a** the whole arm twists inward a great deal. This same movement can occur sequentially, the upper arm 'leading', the lower arm and hand following in turn, **7b**. This could also be written as in **7c**. In **7d** one succession occurs during an inward turn and another during an outward turn. In **7e** a return to normal occurs with no sequential activity. One arm succession can take place while performing an inward and a subsequent outward turn, **7f**. Here the involvement of the upper arm ceases after its initial input and returns to its normal state; the succession passing on to the lower arm and hand as the whole arm ends turned outward.

7.2.   Twisting movements of the arms are more often performed with an inward sequence, **7g**, the extremity initiating the twist and the base part, the upper arm, being the last to join in. Ex. **7h** is comparable to **7g**, but the tips of the fingers lead the twisting action. In this the sense of sequential action is diminished, only the extremity is given importance. Ex. **7i** shows an inward twist and then an outward twist each performed with an inward succession. An inward twist with an inward succession followed by an outward twist with an outward succession, **7j**, are physically easy to perform.

7.3.   **Sequential Twists of the Torso.** When performing a twist in the torso, **7k**, the action starts with each part at the same time; the shoulder line (the extremity) travels farther than the base. The action in the pelvis (the base) ceases first. This same twisting action can happen sequentially; in **7l** the rotation will start in the pelvis which will arrive first at its destination, the waist, chest and shoulder line following in turn. This overall action is familiar from the spiral exercise in the torso found in Graham technique, **7m** (not given in detail here). Conversely, the twisting action can start at the extremity, the upper body turning first and the pelvis being the last to arrive, **7n**. This latter, the more familiar, everyday action, is usually started with the head, hence the pelvis-to-head sign.

7.4.   **Sequential Pivot Turns.** In a similar way a turn of the body-as-a-whole can occur sequentially. In the swivel turn on both feet of **7o** the torso turns as a unit above the feet. But in **7p** the action will start in the legs, continue into the pelvis, waist, chest and up. At the end the torso will be in its normal alignment. More familiar is the inverted sequence of **7q** in which the feet are the last to join in. This progression is used in ice skating as the means of reversing direction, a slight lift of weight at the end of the resulting twist in the torso allows the foot to re-align.

7.5. Another movement articulation would be **7r**, leading with the pelvis; here the focus is on the pelvis, producing a different emphasis. In a similar way the head leading the turn in **7s** places an emphasis on the head which changes the character of the movement.

Sequential Rotations, Twists in the Arm

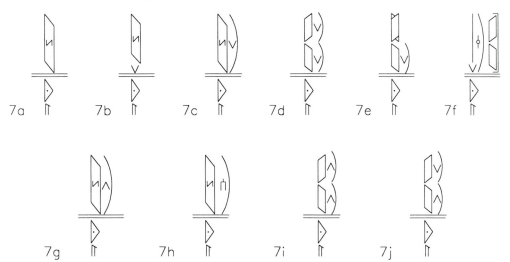

Sequential Twists of the Torso

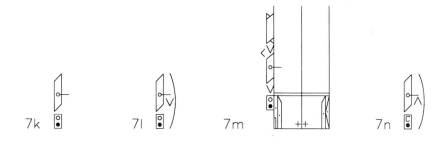

Sequential Pivot Turns

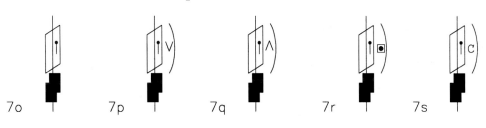

8 Arm Successions with Rotations

8.1.   **Rotations Within the Arm.** The sinewy, apparently boneless arm successions as performed by the Swan Queen in the ballet *Swan Lake*, for example, as well as in Asian Pacific dances and western ballets based on Eastern themes, are the result of rotary actions within the arm combined with successions, rather than rotation (twist) of the arm as a whole. This central rotation is described as a rotation of the elbow, **8a**. To practise this rotation, place the arm sideward, as in **8b**, with the palm facing out (placing the palm against a wall will help stabilize the arm extremity). As the elbow rotates inward and then outward, shoulder and hand should not move. The resulting facing directions for the inside of the elbow have been written alongside **8b** in parentheses to clarify the performance.

8.2.   Such outward rotation can be analyzed as a slight rotation of the upper arm in one direction resulting in a passive rotation of the lower arm in the opposite direction, **8c**. The hand is excluded from such lower arm rotation; this may be expressed as an exclusion of the hand, as in **8d**, or as maintaining the spatial direction of the thumb-edge of the hand, **8e**.

8.3.   The inward elbow rotation of **8f** is more fully indicated as **8g** or **8h**. Note that the degree of elbow rotation is left open; the range is limited but can be somewhat extended through practice. As can be seen, the description in terms of elbow rotation provides a practical abbreviation.

8.4.   **Successions with Upper Arm Rotation.** In **8i** one succession occurs with a slight downward displacement while an outward elbow rotation, ending in an unrotated state takes place. Starting with an inward elbow rotation, as in **8j**, the displacement will be in an upward direction.

8.5.   The movement of **8i** may be embellished by a hand succession occurring at the same time in the opposite direction, **8k**.

Rotations within the Arm

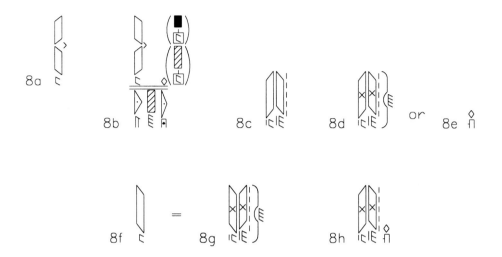

Successions with Upper Arm Rotation

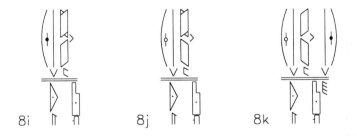

9 Successions, Ripples in the Hand

9.1.   In the arm successions explored in previous sections, the hand has been involved as part of the arm, no particular emphasis was given to it. In **9a** the hand has a succession of its own toward the end of the arm succession thereby producing a distinct, separate hand action.

9.2.   A succession can occur in the hand alone, **9b**. In this example nothing is stated as to whether or not the arm is involved in such successions. The arm may react passively to the hand movements, **9c**, or be specifically excluded, i.e. held still, during the hand succession, **9d**. This exclusion of the arm which makes the hand succession more limited, could also be indicated by use of the exclusion bow, as in **9e**.

9.3.   Exclusion of the wrist in the action can be shown, **9f**. Here the movement is limited to the knuckles in the hand and joints of the fingers, best performed by those with long supple hands. Ex. **9g** shows a succession in the fingers. In **9h** only four fingers are involved, the bulk of the hand and the thumb must remain quiet.

9.4.   The flexibility of the hand together with wrist articulation to accommodate the movement, provide expressive as well as decorative sequential gestures. Small hand successions can become a series of ripples when the movements are fast and occur one following the other, **9i**, in contrast to a single, undulating movement.

9.5.   **Direction of Displacement.** As with the arm, direction of displacement in a hand succession is shown by a pin. In **9j**, with the arm held to the side with the palm down, the hand performs a succession over downward. This occurs in the direction in which the palm is facing. In **9k** the palm is facing up and the succession is over upward. This is the same physical movement for the hand as **9k**, although it feels different. In contrast **9l** is a succession upward, i.e. the direction in which the back of the hand is facing, thus the base of the back of the hand rises at the start instead of the pad at the base of the hand (see Section 4 for direction of displacement).

9.6.   When the arm is static, directions of displacement for the hand are taken from the Standard Cross, **9m**. With the arm in motion, as frequently occurs in Spanish and in Asian Pacific dances, directions must be taken from the Individual Body Part System of Reference[9], **9n**. This key needs to be stated, as in **9o** in which the arm rotates as it changes direction.

9.7.   **Surface Leading.** When leading with the thumb-edge, **9p**, hand flexibility is less; the articulation is mainly in the wrist joint and the base joint of the fingers. The same is true of **9q**, leading with the little finger-edge.

Ripples in the Hand

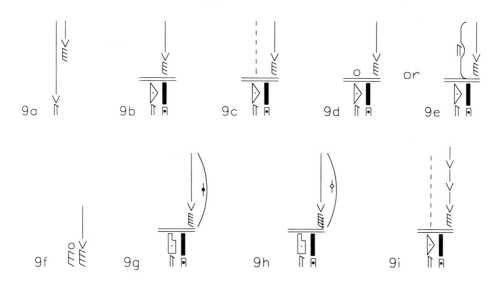

Direction of Displacement

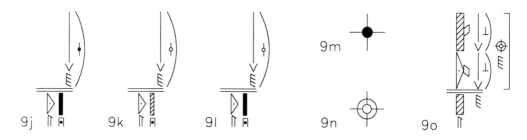

Surface Leading

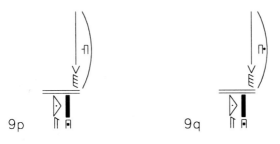

10 Partial Sequence in the Arm

10.1.   Not all sequential movements or successions go through the whole arm, they may end before the hand is involved, i.e. at the wrist, or they may only start at the elbow so that the upper arm is not at all involved. The following method of showing these differences was the contribution of Sigurd Leeder.[10]

10.2.   **Ending Part for a Sequence or Succession.** It is possible, though unusual, for a sequential movement in the arm to terminate at the elbow. With the idea of the flow progressing out from the base of the limb (the part nearest the torso), the indication of the body part where the flow stops is placed (in relation to the staff) on the outer side of the V sign, **10a**. In **10b** the dotted line, used here for explanatory purposes, shows the direction of the flow out to the elbow in relation to the center of the staff. Thus **10c** shows a limited sequential movement as the arm rises to side middle. As the flow starts in the shoulder muscles and the upper arm is involved, the elbow bends slightly, then, the flow being terminated at the elbow, the arm rises to its normal side middle placement. If no shoulder involvement or feeling of flow occurs, this action would be described as being led at first by the elbow, **10d**.

10.3.   Ex. **10e** shows the signs for ending the sequential movement at the wrist; this means there will be no articulation, no succession in the hand, the hand will remain neutral, i.e. merely carried along and passively moving into place at the end. This partial sequential movement, illustrated in **10f**, has the arm rising from down to forward middle. No change of direction is shown in **10g** in which the upward succession finishes at the wrist.

10.4.   Less usual is a succession of the arm which terminates in the hand, i.e. at the base knuckles of the fingers, the fingers themselves not being included. Such a movement can be indicated by the signs of **10h**. In **10i** such limitation occurs when the arm lowers sequentially from up to side middle, the articulation stopping at the fingers; it is performed without action in the hand, as though the fingers are 'asleep'. A similar action occurs in **10j** during an upward arm succession.

10.5.   **Origin of an Outward Sequential Movement, Succession.** In exploring variations in arm successions, one finds that often the upper arm takes little, if any, part. This can be particularly true when rotations (twists) occur (see Section 7). As a result the sequential movement may start from the elbow and progress out from there. An outward sequence starting from the elbow is indicated by adding the elbow sign to the *inner side of the V sign*, **10k**; the origin (the elbow sign) being closer to the center line of the staff. In this placement it shows *from where the movement originates*, from where it flows out. In **10l** a succession starts at the elbow as the arm moves from forward to the side. A similar succession, **10m**, occurs without a spatial change.

10.6.   The wrist may be the source for the succession, as in **10n**. In **10o** the arm starts sideward and lowers with a succession involving only the wrist, hand and fingers. No spatial change occurs in **10p** for the upward succession starting in the wrist. In all of these examples the rest of the arm should not actively take part in the sequential movement.

Ending Part for a Sequential Movement, Succession

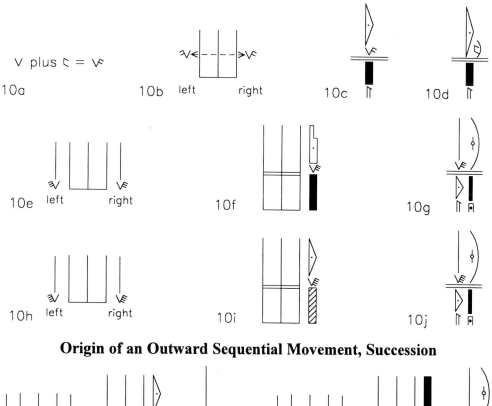

Origin of an Outward Sequential Movement, Succession

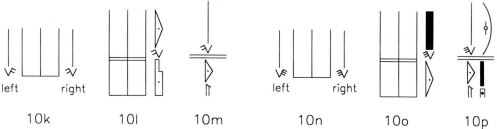

11   Central Sequential Movements

11.1.   As mentioned before, in an ordinary arm succession, such as **11a**, the undulation starts with the shoulder muscles, the upper arm being displaced first. Note that there is virtually no spatial displacement of the shoulder. In the Jooss-Leeder technique students learned to differentiate between a slight central movement in which the initiation came from the shoulder, a more marked central initiation in which the shoulder area is involved, and the deeper central movement in which the motion emanates from the center of the torso, the waist or solar plexus.[11]

11.2.   If the shoulder itself is visibly 'engaged' (a slight displacement) at the start of the sequential movement, the shoulder sign is added to the V sign to indicate the starting point, **11b**. This shoulder displacement, which increases the visible effect of the movement, disappears as the succession flows through the arm, returning to normal about a third-way through. Such movement could be emotionally based, the shoulders being 'the thermometer of passion' according to François Delsarte.[12] Ex. **11c** illustrates this usage. In **11d** this central sequential action occurs as the arm rises to the side. This could also be written as **11e**, the sign being placed within the vertical bow. It should be noted that leading with the shoulder, as in **11f**, produces a larger movement in which the shoulder 'juts out' at the start.

11.3.   Involvement of the **shoulder area** increases the central expression. The muscles of that quarter of the chest are brought into play at the start, subsiding as the flow moves on. This stage of central involvement is written with a dot placed within the V sign, **11g**.[13] Ex. **11h**, a succession, and **11i** and **11j**, sequential movements, show this degree of central initiation used for the right arm. Such central initiation disappears soon after the sequential flow is on its way.

11.4.   Carrying this further, the movement can originate at the center of the torso providing a central 'outpouring'. Interpretation of this is usually similar to taking in a breath, the flow of the movement originating at the base of the chest, or perhaps the waist. Such initiation enriches the sequential arm gesture and may maximise its emotional basis.[14] This central initiation will inevitably vary from one performer to another; detailed use of the torso can be spelled out when needed. Such central movements tend to produce a larger sequential movement.

11.5.   The general statement for this central initiation is to place a small x within the V sign, **11k**.[15] This x relates to the waist sign, the 'center' of the torso. In **11l** the right arm performs a succession originating from this area of the body. In **11m** the arm moves from down to side middle with such deep central initiation. This movement could also be written as **11n**.

11.6.   The same usage for central sequences can be applied to a leg gesture. Ex. **11o** gives the signs for starting a succession from the hip. In **11p** this is applied to a forward low gesture. Greater lower torso involvements are shown in **11q** and **11r**. Note the difference between these and the following: in **11s** the sequential gesture is shown to be led at first by the hip. The more outspoken focus on a part leading is different from the source of an outward sequence.

Central Sequential Movements

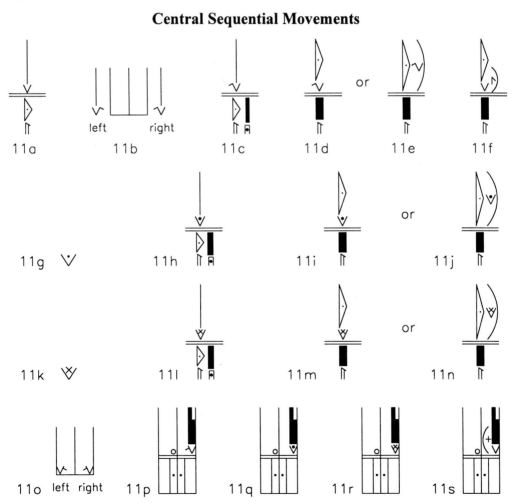

12 Sequential Movements for the Torso

12.1.   **Sequential Torso Movements on the Floor.** When a directional movement occurs for the whole torso, instead of the torso tilting as a unit, the manner of performance may be sequential in that the change of direction starts at the base of the torso and concludes at the extremity. Ex. **12a** describes the commonly met way of lying down from sitting, illustrated in **12b**. Similarly **12c** describes the usual, expected way of sitting up from lying on the back, illustrated in **12d**. The reverse, starting the sequence with the extremity when moving from sitting to lying backward, **12e**, illustrated in **12f**, is far from comfortable and, indeed, not very good for the lower back. Similarly, sitting up by first lifting the base of the spine, **12g**, illustrated in **12h**, is less familiar and may also impose a strain on the lower back.

12.2.   **Sequential Torso Movements while Standing.** The previous examples are also applicable to the upright standing situation. Ex. **12i** (which can also be written as **12j**) is a fairly familiar way of moving sequentially to forward middle, while **12k** is a very usual and comfortable manner of returning to upright. Performed in sequence, the two produce an undulating wave through the spine, often done as an exercise while facing the barre and holding onto it.

12.3.   In **12l** an inward sequence is used. This action may be experienced more as the head leading the change of direction for the torso, **12m**. Such leading action of the head usually finishes before the main movement is completed, thus the head returns to its normal alignment. Because the vertical bow terminates about halfway before the end of the main movement, the head leading terminates sooner, it returns to normal. The effect of **12m** is to produce less of a sequence through the whole spine. When rising from forward middle to upright the change in direction can also be performed as an inward sequence, **12n**. Here again, this performance may more easily be felt as one in which the head leads the movement, **12o**, but the wave-like flow from the periphery inward is lost. In Section 17 variations on inward successions are explored (see Sections 17 and 18 for sideward torso sequences and sequences for part of the torso and for augmented torso).

Sequential Torso Movements on the Floor

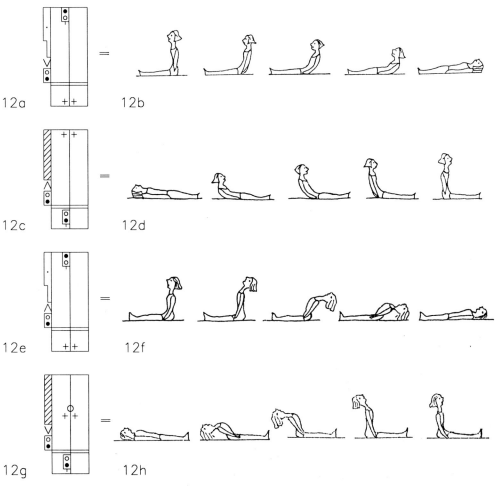

12a 12b

12c 12d

12e 12f

12g 12h

Sequential Torso Movements while Standing

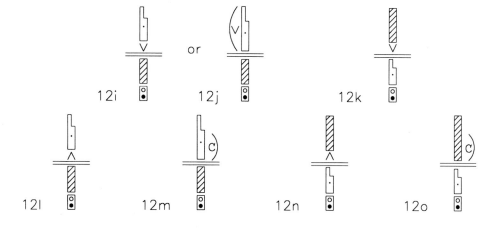

12i or 12j 12k

12l 12m 12n 12o

13 Successions in the Torso

13.1.　　Without changing direction, successions (undulations) can occur in the torso. Such undulations often happen when the torso is upright. The following examples will take an understood upright stance for which outward successions will be explored.

13.2.　　When there is no basic change of direction, successions in the torso, i.e. through the spine, bring up the question of where the movement ends. To what extent is the head involved? As a rule, in our analysis the head and neck are treated as a unit, however, the cranium (the skull) which sits on the Atlas, the last vertebrae, may or may not make a movement of its own at the start or at the finish of a succession through the torso. If the neck and cranium are to be included, the symbol of **13a** should be used. The following examples, however, deal with the general usage of the whole torso.

13.3.　　**Outward Succession.** Ex. **13b** shows a single outward succession, no particular manner of performance has been stated. To achieve a succession a slight displacement must take place. In **13c** this displacement is designated as being forward. If the movement is small, a slight forward shift occurs first at the base, the pelvis, and travels up the torso, ending at the neck. The head (skull) will react passively, without making any special motion of its own. If the movement is larger, it may involve a slight tilt and/or a slight backward somersault of the head. As the forward displacement travels up the spine, the lower part resumes its normal alignment. In **13d** the displacement is to the left side, thus the left hip will jut out very slightly as the pelvis displaces in that direction, the succession continuing through the waist, chest and neck. In the sideward direction, articulation at the waist is more difficult and the chest soon takes over; however, the effect of a successive ripple is achieved. While standing, successions can occur into any of the horizontal directions around the body, the appropriate pin being used.

13.4.　　With the body in different situations, such as lying down, **13e**, the direction of the deviation can be different. The forward deviation in **13c** is now a deviation upward, according to the Standard directions. If the Body Key is used, as in **13f**, the direction of deviation would be forward. When standing, the physical directions are the same for both Standard and the Body Keys.

13.5.　　**Degree of Displacement.** Precision in successions is not usually required. Performances will vary; usually very fine delineations are not needed. However, a general idea of size can be given by use of a measurement sign within the diamond representing space thus providing a general statement regarding the use of space. Such indications, useful for arm successions, may be particularly needed for the size of torso movements. Ex. **13g** states spatially large; **13h** spatially very large. A small use of space is shown in **13i** and spatially very small in **13j**. Each of these indications is relative; no precise measurement is given. In **13k** the forward displacement is shown to be large, in **13l** very large. The signs for size can be placed within the bow as in **13m** which shows a small forward succession for the torso. In **13n** the diagonal succession is to be very small.

Successions in the Torso

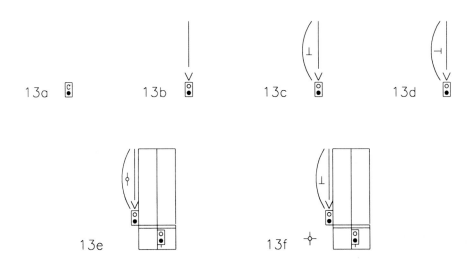

Degree of Displacement

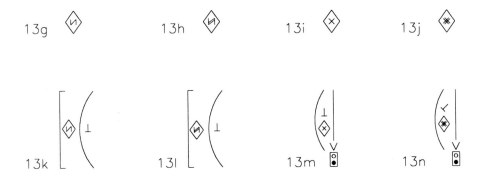

14 Sequential Movements for Contracting, Folding

14.1.   In the following examples the torso is understood to start in the upright situation. Contracting the whole torso, as in **14a**, occurs as a single movement; the parts of the spine curve simultaneously. Note that, when nothing is stated, the contraction is understood to be over the front surface. Such a contraction can commence at the base and conclude at the shoulder line, **14b**. Or, conversely, the upper spine can begin and the movement can flow down to the base, **14c**. For each of these the end result is the same.

14.2.   In a similar way the spine can lengthen, elongate, all parts moving simultaneously, **14d**. Or the elongation can start at the base, **14e**, or at the extremity, **14f**. At the end of these examples the torso will be stretched. If the natural, non-stretched state of the spine is wanted, then the sign for neither-stretched-nor-bent, **14g**, can be used.

14.3.   Folding the torso, **14h**, can also be performed sequentially with an outward flow, as in **14i**, the shoulder line being the last to arrive, or with an inward flow, as in **14j**, which starts in the upper spine.

14.4.   As mentioned in Section 13, in movements of the whole torso the head follows passively. If, however, it is actively to take part, the sign for pelvis-to-head as a unit should be used, as in **14k** and **14l** where a sequential unfolding takes place (see Reading Examples).

14.5.   An arm may move from a stretched position to a spatially closed position, the normal manner of performance being for the parts of the arm to move to the new location at the same time, unison action, **14m**. In **14n** this same movement is performed with an outward sequence, the upper arm will begin, the lower arm following and the hand coming to rest only at the end.

14.6.   The reverse is true in **14o**, the hand moves first to its destination, the rest of the arm following; the elbow will be the last to come to rest.

14.7.   Moving from a spatially closed position to a stretched state is shown in **14p**; all parts of the arm will open out and travel to the new destination in unison. The performance of **14q** is the comfortable, familiar outward sequential movement to the destination. But a very different feeling and expression is produced in **14r** for which the hand starts the 'journey', the upper arm being the last to come into its destination. It should be noted that in performing these sequential examples some degree of arm rotation may be required, but is not stressed.

Sequential Movements for Contracting, Folding

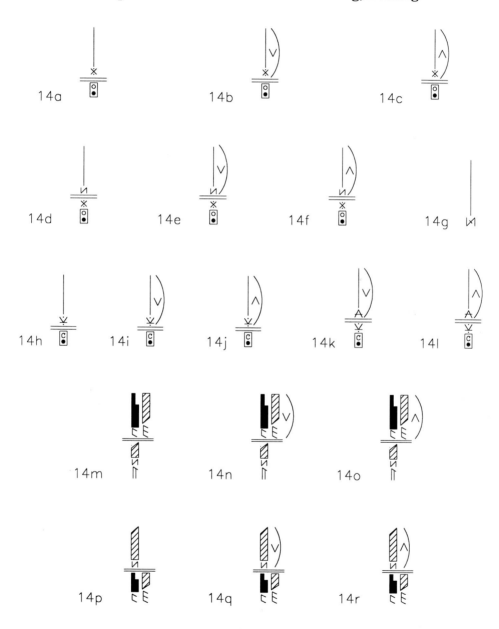

15 Body Waves

15.1.   *Body waves*, which are often called *impulses* when performed swiftly and with a forceful burst of energy at the start, were a feature of European modern dance during the 20s and 30s.[16] A body wave is a sequential movement through the spine which is greatly augmented spatially so that it includes action in the legs as well as in the arms. Such a wave starts from the base of the torso (the pelvis), and this enlarged sequential movement, usually circular in design, passes through the spine until it is dissipated. Body waves can be quite slow and sustained; they usually involve the whole body, but can be more locally active. Such movements were also a feature of Isadora Duncan's style, a movement flowing through the whole body from an inner source and emanating, escaping through the extremities. Most body waves are outward flowing sequences although inward sequences can also occur. Displacement in space may vary from slight to considerable. There are many subtle ways in which such body waves can be performed, and each can be spelled out in specific detail when such precision is needed. However, if only the general idea is needed, this can be stated quite simply.

15.2.   For those familiar with this form of movement, the general statement of **15a**, can be made. The double V sign across the whole staff indicates that all of the body, including the arms, is involved. Doubling the V sign gives the message of "More!" Also, the double V cannot be confused with an increase sign. The length of the double V gives the duration which includes the preparatory movements. In this example no direction is indicated for the body wave. For those unfamiliar with this form of movement, an explanatory introduction and a full description are given here as well as the abbreviated form.

15.3.   **Direction of a Body Wave.** Ex. **15b** shows a body wave over forward. The single direction sign in the double V states the direction of the main thrust. The direction sign is centered within the double V and is not placed in one or other support column. The center line is eliminated where the symbol appears. For a full body wave the preparation needs to be in opposite direction to the main thrust. In the case of **15b** this preparation would be backward. The preparation and follow-through as well as the normal body alignment to be achieved at the end are understood to take place within the timing given for the action. The degree of articulation - the size of displacement, the degree of preparation, and the degree of lowering to produce the full circular movement - can vary according to the person's build, flexibility and range of previous movement experience.

15.4.   **Standard Description of a Forward Body Wave.** In **15c** a full circular forward body wave is spelled out. It is given here as it was taught at the Jooss-Leeder school, at the Folkwang Hochschule in Essen, and at the Wigman School in Dresden. Different versions of body waves in which the overall spatial pattern is modified may have developed elsewhere. The body is lowered through a deep *plié* and the pelvis carried backward as the whole torso leans forward. At the depth of the *plié* the pelvis comes in line over the feet as the curved torso also comes in line (the shoulders above the hips). From here the pelvis thrusts forward as far as possible while the torso 'unfolds' sequentially in the opposite direction. As the pelvis returns to its normal alignment, the waist and the chest in turn complete the forward sequential circle before returning to alignment. The head, which has only been a passive participant in the action, moving as a result of the spinal action, also returns to normal.

15.5.   In a full body wave the pelvis performs the overall spatial pattern of a large sagittal circular path; in **15c** this is a backward somersault pathway. While the notation of **15c** should produce this, the notation does not convey the smooth, continuous pelvic action which contributes to the flow of the body wave. Therefore, the path of the pelvis, **15d**, can be added to the notation to convey this idea directly.

Body Wave

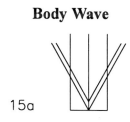

15a

Forward Body Wave

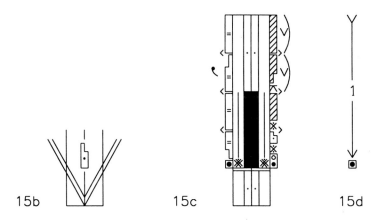

15b   15c   15d

15.6.   **Body waves in Different Directions.** Body waves can be performed in different directions. Ex. **15e** illustrates a body wave over backward. For each body wave the preparation is in the opposite direction to the main thrust. Thus, for a backward body wave the pelvis will prepare by moving forward, as the torso folds backward.

15.7.   Ex. **15f** and **15g** show body waves to sideward left, and diagonally forward left respectively. For **15f** the preparation will be to the right side. The pelvis will shift to the right to start the circular body wave, become centered as the movement continues down, then move to the left before returning to centre. The torso counterbalances, as in the body waves described above. During this sequence the pelvis makes a cartwheeling path. For practising this sideward wave, it is helpful to grasp the barre with the right hand.

15.8.   **Waves Stressing More Than One Direction.** Though every body wave has one principal direction, other directions can be given importance by writing more than one direction symbol within the body wave sign. In **15h** the downward motion should be stressed during the forward body wave. The backward direction is also to be given importance in **15i**.

15.9.   Other aspects of a body wave can also be specified in the notation. Ex. **15j** shows starting on half-toe and rising at the end of the body wave thus augmenting the feeling of a large circular movement. This general indication is spelt out in **15k** in which, halfway through the movement, the body is in a deep *plié* and the ending returns again to the high half-toe, the body upright and elongated to get the fullest value. Any raising of the heels during lowering, and the moment of stretching the legs on rising are not stated, one achieves the overall pattern without stressing details.

15.10.   **One-Sided Emphasis.** While it is not physically possible to separate right and left sides of the torso, particularly of the pelvis, the focus, the initiation, the emphasis can be on one side. These are, of course, general statements. In **15l** the forward body wave emphasises the left side of the body. More emphasis, more energy will be given to that side and probably the left arm will be featured. The same is true of **15m** in which the right side is featured in the sideward right body wave. This example contrasts with **15f** where the sense is more of an involvement of the whole body.

Body Waves in Different Directions

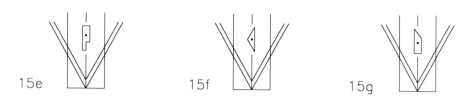

15e   15f   15g

Waves Streeing More Tahn One Direction

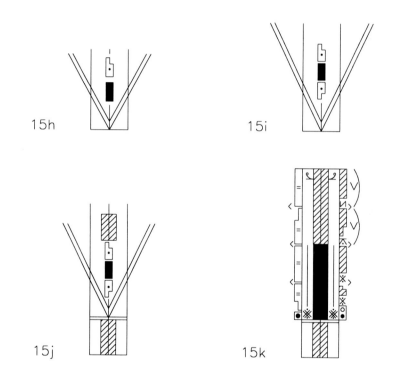

15h   15i

15j   15k

One-sided Emphasis

15l   15m

15.11.   **Indicating Body Wave Action.** When the movement is carefully
spelled out in detailed notation, the sense of flow and continuity of a
successional body wave can be added to express the sense of the movement.
The double V can be placed in a vertical bracket as in **15n** and placed alongside
a movement sequence, **15o**. However, the double V can also be placed across
the definitive movement description, **15p**. The sign gives an immediate
message as to the type of movement wanted. Exs. **15o** and **15p** both show a
body wave into the diagonal forward left direction.

15.12.   **Sequential Actions Added.** The manner of performance can be
augmented by adding sequential movements for the torso. Such sequential
movements will result in greater spinal articulation. In the forward body wave
of **15q** a sequential movement sign is shown toward the end of the sequence as
the torso folds backward and then comes upright. The forward displacement of
the pelvis is stressed to alert the performer to the importance of giving full value
to this part of the circle. The shifting forward articulation of the pelvis is more
difficult to perform than the backward shift.

15.13.   In the backward body wave of **15r** three sequential actions occur,
the first on the backward folding, another on the movement passing through
upright to forward folding and the third on the return to upright. This last will
be experienced over the back surface of the torso. A slow movement allows for
such specificity. Although the changes in direction are analyzed here as three
separate sequential movements, if performed at speed, one overall sign could be
used instead as a general statement, **15s**, because the experience is of one
continuous succession. To achieve the full potential of the movement, these
body waves can be practised at the barre, either with one hand on the barre, or
facing the barre using both hands.

Indicating Body Wave Action

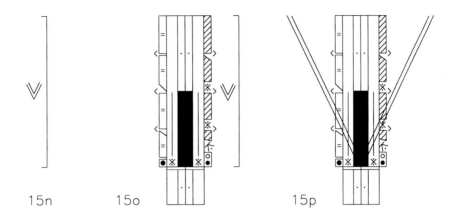

15n   15o   15p

Sequential Actions Added

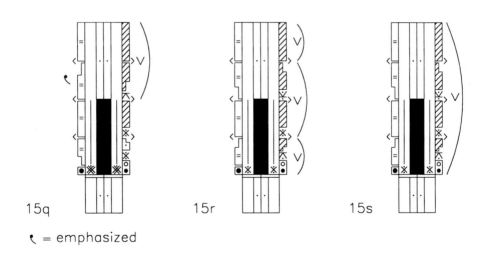

15q   15r   15s

ʕ = emphasized

16 Impulse in the Body

16.1.　　As the name suggests, an 'impulse' starts with an outburst of energy which dissipates as the movement progresses, the sudden start changing to an increasingly sustained movement. In **16a** a strong accent is shown at the start and the indication for diminishing speed is given alongside.[17] A spatially large impulse is spelled out in **16b**, the preparatory pelvic movement backward and downward being shown not to be stressed, the accent being on the forward motion.

16.2.　　In contrast, **16c** shows a slow body wave over forward which ends with the chest arched (folded) backward.

16.3.　　Such body waves and impulses are not always trained to great specificity, a range of individual interpretation is often allowed.

Impulse in the Body

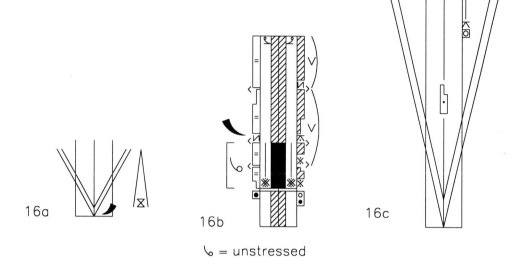

16a   16b   16c

↳ = unstressed

17 Examples of Inward Sequential Movements

17.1.   While inward sequential movements,[18] successions, and body waves are less familiar than outward ones, there are several interesting examples to explore here. The first, **17a**, is a pattern taken from Street Dancing.[19] An inward succession for the right arm flows through the body and on out through the left arm. In this example the accompanying head and chest shifts augment the effect. Performed smoothly, the action can be snake-like. One can also imagine a ball rolling from the hand to the shoulder and then across to the other arm.

17.2.   A snake-like movement through the spine takes place in **17b** moving from the head through to the pelvis and returning to upright with the head again changing direction first. This spinal undulation can also be performed with some overlap so that the return to upright starts sooner, **17c** (see Section 6 for overlapping sequences).

17.3.   An inward sequential change of direction occurs in the process of lying down forward onto the front of the body. Ex. **17d** is taken from Doris Humphrey's *Water Study*.[20] From the kneeling position at the start, the head-to-pelvis unit moves with an inward sequence, head, shoulders and chest going first into the forward direction leading into lying prone. As this takes place, the palms slide forward along the floor. The vibrating (rippling) finger actions are explained in the original score. (See Section 12 for sequential torso movements, ex. **12l** occurs here in **17d**.)

Examples of Inward Sequential Movements

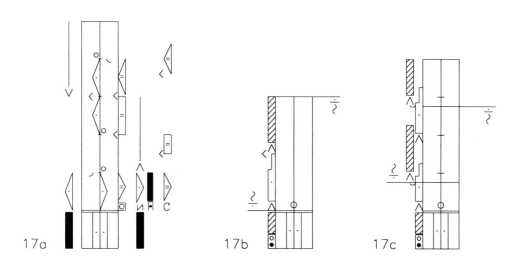

17a   17b   17c

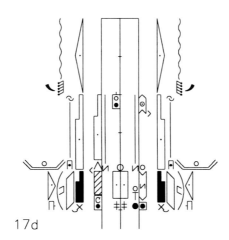

17d

17.4.   An increasing use of the parts of the torso can occur in conjunction with another movement. Ex. **17e** spells out a movement which starts with the head and then, in succession, includes the shoulder section, chest and the augmented chest. During the knee bend in second position the head makes a circular pattern which involves an increasing amount of the upper torso, an inward sequence.

17.5.   In **17f** this sequential involvement of the torso is indicated through an inclusion bow together with an inward sequence (i.e. starting with the extremity) for the unit of waist-to-chest. This head circle is described in **17g** with a circular path sign as well as the inward successive use of the body. This description has the advantage of showing the circling activity more directly but, as written, does not include the rotation for the head which augments the feeling of the circular path.

17.6.   The result of this successive inclusion of the body is that the head describes a spiralling path, as can be seen from above. While **17e** and **17f** spell out the movement of the body parts, the important concept in this sequence is stated more directly in **17g**. Ex. **17h** states the outward spiral described by the head more directly; but how this is achieved may still need to be indicated.

17.7.   In a similar way to the above examples, the sequence of parts of the torso involved in changing a basic position can be indicated. In **17i**, from lying on the back, the body is raised up starting from the extremity, the feet, until it is resting only on the upper back of the shoulder section, illustrated in **17j**. This action might be described as being led by the feet, **17k**, but the sense of (and striving for) a sequential participation in the parts of the torso would be missed.

17.8.   The forward and upward body wave of **17l** starts in a crouch and ends with supports and arms in high level (see Section 15 for body waves). The reversal of this movement, **17m**, should be a retracing of the same path in the reverse direction. It will be found that physically it is difficult, if not impossible, to achieve a comparable sequence; the sense of a body wave is not really there. It is for this reason that body waves are usually outflowing patterns. In attempting to perform **17l** as a wave it is probable that **17n** will be performed, a gradual collapsing, starting with the extremities, the hands and head; such a sequential movement does not have the sense or impact of a body wave.

Examples of Inward Sequential Movements (cont)

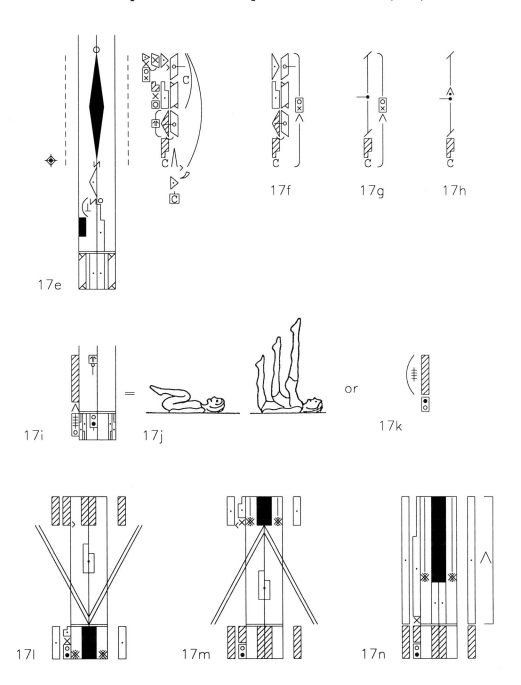

17e

17f

17g

17h

17i

17j

or

17k

17l

17m

17n

18 Reading Examples

18.1.   The following reading examples, taken from existing notations have been updated and adopted where need be to meet the needs in this book. The meaning of some signs, mainly dynamic signs, have been included where need be.[21]

18.2.   **Body Waves with Accompanying Arm Movements.** Use of the arms during a body wave may vary; the following simple examples are taken from Jooss-Leeder technique. When practicing at the barre, the free arm was used either to follow the circle of the body wave or to move in opposition. The more familiar form for sagittal body waves was to use the arm in opposition as shown in **18a** for a forward wave; however, **18b** for the same body wave was also quite common. The same is true for the body wave over backward (reverse sagittal circle) as in **18c**. In this example the arm is shown to move sequentially in the forward section of the circle.

18.3.   For a lateral circle over the left or right side, when the arm follows the same circle, it starts with the elbow leading strongly across to the other side, the arm then unfolds sequentially downward and outward on its way to completing the circle, **18d**. A sequential arm movement encompassing two directions means that the arm is still bent while passing through the first direction and only extends normally as it arrives at the second direction, its destination.

18.4.   When moving in opposition, **18e**, the sequential part occurs at the end with sufficient inward rotation to accomplish the movement smoothly. When these body waves are performed with both arms they may move symmetrically or in opposition.

Reading Examples

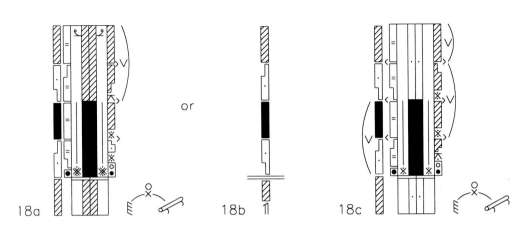

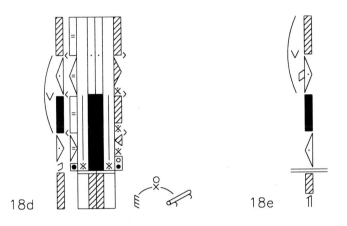

18.5.   **Humphrey Sideward Sequential Movements.**[22] The sideward sequential movement of **18f**, again Humphrey technique, shows several elements which add to the wave-like character of this exercise in which the chest-to-waist section moves sequentially from side to side. The indication of the chest leading with pressure, followed with increasing relaxation into a sideward fold, is full of dynamic coloring. The shift of the center of weight from side to side, which results when one knee bends and the other straightens, augments the spatial displacement. In the second part of the exercise the arm movement further augments the look and the feel of these sequential body movements.

18.6.   **Humphrey Sagittal Sequential Movement.**[23] Ex. **18g** shows sequential folding and unfolding of the torso and of the section from knees-to-chest in the forward and backward directions. From a lifted starting position, the feet in a narrow high 4th, the performer first arches backward, the arms rotating as they move forward high, then the body lowers to a deep *plié*, the torso folding forward sequentially. It then unfolds backward with a forward pelvic shift as the whole body starts to rise, the sweeping backward circle of the arms enlarges the movement. Because of the symmetry produced by both arms moving forward when going down and backward on the rising and backward arch, there is no rotation in the rib cage.

Reading Examples (cont)

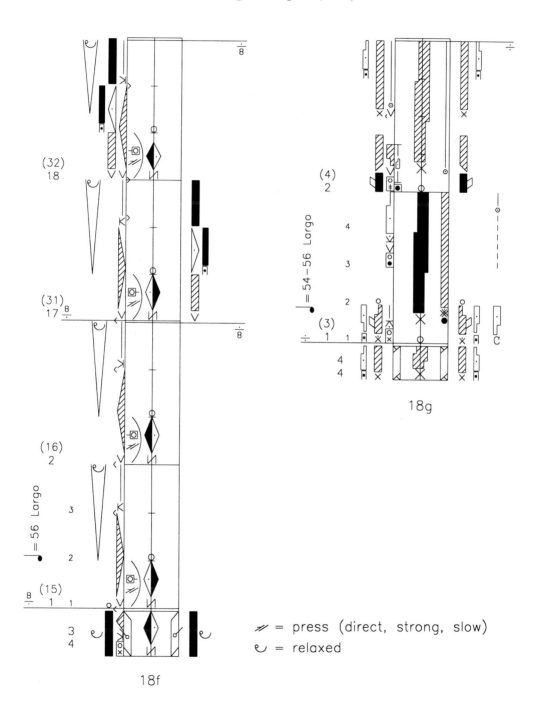

18f

18g

♩♩ = press (direct, strong, slow)

ʊ = relaxed

18.7.   **'Falls'.** The next two examples describe the centered, 'waves breaking on a shore' type of fall. In these no real loss of balance takes place, that is, no falling action in which the center of weight markedly moves beyond the point of support. In this type of 'fall' the weight is centered as the body lowers, the upper body leaning away from the direction of the fall to control balance. Once weight is taken on the hip(s), the torso and arms 'unfold', the arm(s) sliding along the floor like a wave breaking on the shore. Ex. **18h** shows a side fall as taught by Ted Shawn.[24] The action of lowering the torso to the floor will tend naturally to be performed sequentially. However, the performer should give full value to this sequential movement as well as to the augmented chest tilt away from the direction of the fall. This tilt and the arm circle in the same direction, provide the counter balance needed for a smooth lowering to the floor so that no jarring moment or loss of balance occurs. Again, the circling motion of the arms enlarge the look and feel of the successive movement.

18.8.   **Backward Fall and Recovery from Humphrey's First Series of Falls.**[25] In **18i** the initial downward swing of the arms and forward fold of the chest lead into the upward spring which is assisted by the forward and upward arm swing which propel the body into motion. The forward bending of the torso at the start of the backward fall helps control the lowering as does the weight being taken on the hands as the arms slide 'backward'. The sequential backward torso movement also softens the process of lying down. For the recovery the torso rises with a sequential movement, the sternum leading into the upright position. The torso then folds forward as the weight is transferred to the left knee and the right foot, these leading into coming upright as the arms move sagittally up to return to the starting position. (See Section 12 and 14 for discussion of this type of movement.)

Reading Examples (cont)

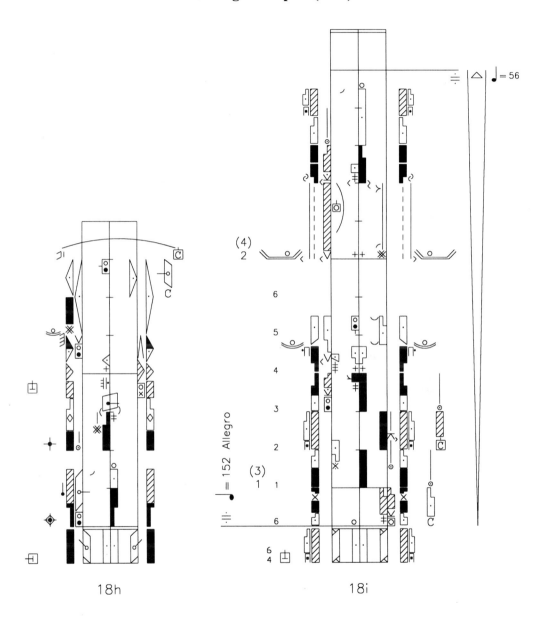

18h   18i

18.9.   **Hand Ripples.** A measure from *Incense* by Ruth St. Denis is
shown in **18j**.[26] The movements in the notation happen after the dancer has
moved diagonally left to the Incense Burner, holding a bowl with incense in the
left hand, and has grasped some incense from the bowl with the right thumb and
middle finger. The notation shows that the incense is released from the fingers
above the Incense Burner as the right hand ripples three times. At the same time
the torso 'opens' (rotates) toward this hand, and the torso and right arm rise
upward, thus contributing to the expression of smoke rising and spiralling (see
Section 9 for a discussion of hand ripples).

18.10.   The key given for this traditional Hawaiian Dance, called *Lovely
Hula Hands*,[27] is of slight leg flexion for each step. The focus throughout is on
the hand motions. At the start both arms move to left where the hands perform
a succession over downward and upward. The hands again perform a ripple on
count 3 as the arms cross in front of the body, palms facing backward. During
this first measure the step pattern is to the right. On each step the hip sway is
produced by the free foot (that relinquishing weight) pushing up onto the ball of
the foot, thus causing the hip on that side to rise. Note that the lifting of one hip
automatically cancels the previous lift of the other hip. This first measure is
then repeated to the other side. The 3rd measure starts with both arms sideward,
two degrees bent and thumb edges facing forward. First the right arm reaches
out to normal extension while the hands, undulate (moving side high, side low,
ending side middle), the fingertips leading. The same gesture is performed by
the left arm and hand during the second half of the measure. Note the overcurve
steps from side to side. In measure 4, during three small forward steps, the arms
start forward, palms facing down, and then draw in as the hands perform a
downward and upward ripple. The arms continue to move in, ending with the
hands above the shoulders where they perform a downward succession. The
head and eyes follow the hands most of the time.

Reading Examples (cont)

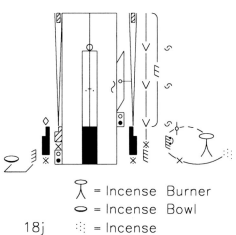

Ⳟ = Incense Burner
◯ = Incense Bowl
18j   ⁞⁞⁞ = Incense

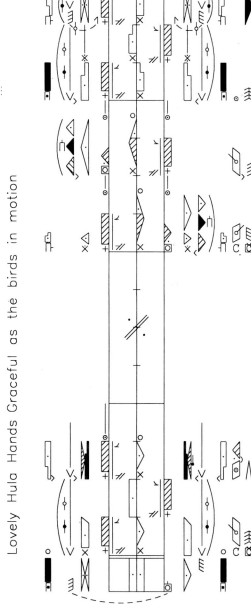

Lovely Hula Hands Graceful as the birds in motion

key =

18k

18.11.   **Partial Sequential Movements for the Arm.** In **18l** the dancer
steps out three times, each time a bit further away from the other foot. With
each step the arm moves a bit further up with a sequential movement, this
involves parts of the arm which each time are closer to the extremity. (See
Section 10 for partial sequential movement.) In the first arm movement the
involvement of the shoulder is emphasized and the flow continues only until the
elbow; the wrist and hand move passively to their destination. Next the arm
moves with a sequential movement activated only as far as the wrist; the hand
passively moves to its destination. During the last step a sequential movement
starting from the elbow flows outward through the rest of the arm.

18.12.   **Central Sequential Movements for the Arm.** In **18m**, shown
below, an arm exercise from Jooss-Leeder technique is shown.[28] This notation
shows overlapping sequential arm movements in which the shoulder is involved
in the movements (see Section 10 for partial sequences in the arm and Section 6
for overlapping sequences). Thus, the part near the base of the arm already
starts moving down when the extremity of the arm is still on its way up. Ex.
18n shows the same pattern performed in a more central way, the shoulder area
being involved in both the sideward and downward parts of the movement (see
Section 11 for central sequential movements).

18.13.   **Sequential Movement of the Leg.** In **18o** another sequential leg
movement from Jooss-Leeder technique is shown. The leg lifts to the side and
then returns down, only one sequential action taking place for both directions,
starting with the thigh and ending with the foot contacting the floor. It is to be
performed with relaxation ending with total relaxation, a 'flop' (see Section 3
for sequential movements of the leg).

Reading Examples (cont)

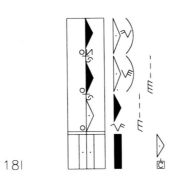

18l

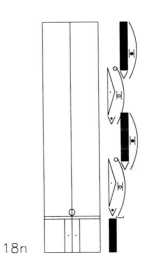

18m   18n

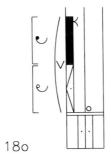

18o   ⌣ = very relaxed

                                       ᴜ = relaxed

18.14.   Ex. **18p** is an arm exercise from the technique of Asadata Dafora as taught by Marcia Heard.[29] The four base knuckles of the fingers start contracted two degrees.[30] Variation I shows a succession through the hand flowing out through the fingers as the hand stretches down. In Variation II the wrist action is included, folding backward as the knuckles contract and then returning to normal extension during the sequential action of the hand. In III the contraction of the knuckles is replaced by a full folding of the hand; the wrist folds to four sides, starting with ulna flexion, then forward, radial, and backward flexion in a circular way. These wrist movements combined with inward and outward rotation of the lower arm produce a gathering-like action followed by unfolding of the hand (no sense of scattering occurs). In Variation IV all the actions of III occur augmented by a slight inward rotation of the elbow which brings it slightly 'forward' in feeling, though the direction is actually sideward. This is followed by a slight outward rotation as the elbow returns to its normal downward placement. Note that for IV the hand movement is not emphasized. In Variation V a shoulder circle is added, yet further augmenting the basic movement. The hand, wrist, and elbow movements remain the same as the shoulder moves forward, upward, back, and down. This circle 'causes' the elbow to contract 45 degrees on the first part,[31] it then returns to normal as the shoulder circle is completed. Again, the hand movement is not to be emphasized.

For versions IV and V Dafora preferred for the hand unfolding the style given in the notation above the staff, in which the hand should not end stretched. It is usual in performance for a succession to unfold in such a way that the ends of the fingers appear to be pointing into the spatial direction, an 'active' conclusion of the movement. Dafora unfolds the succession up to the fingers, the point where the fingers are still folded; then the last part, the unfolding of the hand to return to normal alignment, is unemphasized.

Reading Examples (cont)

preferred style for
unfolding of the
hand in IV and V:

18p   Asadata Dafora exercise

18.15.   **Torso Succession.** Again, an example from Jooss-Leeder Technique is shown in **18q** below. This exercise for the torso starts with the torso and arms stretching forward, both hands holding the barre. The torso performs an outward succession, the displacement occurring first upward and then downward as shown by the pins. The measurement sign at the left indicates that spatially the movement should be large. During the first part the back of the waist rises; during the second part the front of the waist lowers. The head reacts passively (see Section 13 for torso succession).

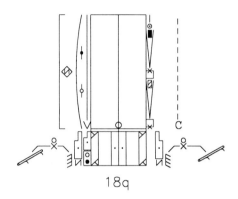

18q

18.16.   **Body Waves.** The examples of body waves given here are from notated dance techniques which feature this form of movement. (Body waves are described in detail in Section 15.)   A forward body wave from the technique of Ted Shawn is shown in **18r**.[32] The sequence goes from a marked reaching up to a low contracted torso situation. This range is further emphasised through the dynamic qualities of heaviness and uplift shown at the right of the staff. The preparatory jumps and arm swings contrast with the powerful forward body wave which follows.

18.17.   Ex. **18s** shows a series of accelerating body waves taken from Shawn technique. The forward thrust takes the performer off balance, weight being caught on a low step forward as the torso bends forward low, preparing for the next body wave. On each 'collapse' the dynamic changes from heavy to relaxed (limp). As the speed increases, the performer catches the weight on one foot after the other, the rise and fall in the footwork coordinating with the waves in the body which cannot now be as full as before.

Reading Examples (cont)

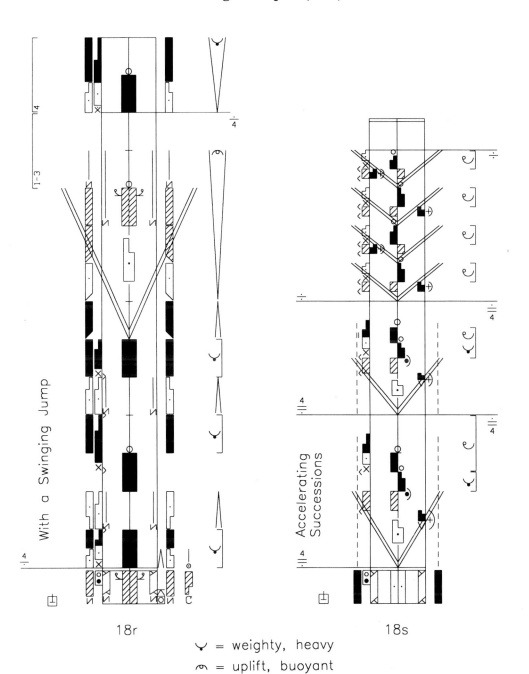

18r

With a Swinging Jump

18s

Accelerating Successions

◡ = weighty, heavy

◠ = uplift, buoyant

ℯ = relaxed

18.18.   The glossary for the notation score of *Water Study* by Doris Humphrey[33] gives the general indications for an overall marked contracted position and the body wave which follows, **18t**, and then explains in detail the correct performance of these movements, **18u**. The body wave in this case consists of a forward shift of the pelvis, the chest arched backward sequentially, and circling of the arms. The lifted end position, emphasized by the Effort sign for 'light' contrasts with the low crouched position that precedes it.

18.19.   In **18v**, which comes from the full score, the movement abbreviation of **18t** is shown in context. It is preceded by a sideward sequential movement of the torso, accompanied by a step and arm movements in the same direction. The dancer then turns and prepares with the torso and arms moving forward before performing the contraction and body wave mentioned above. Note the triangular Time Sign placed within the arm and torso direction symbols to show a slowing down within that gesture.[34] This excerpt is a good illustration of the wave-like character of the movements in *Water Study*.

Reading Examples (cont)

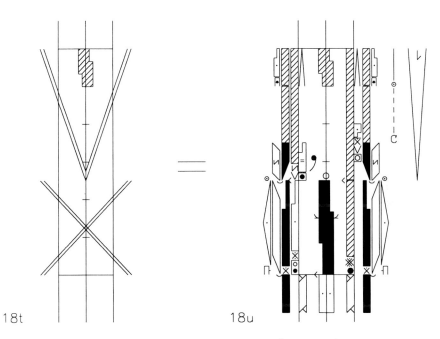

18t   18u

𝄒 = emphasized

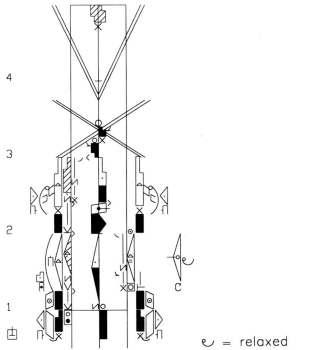

18v   ᴗ = relaxed

Appendix: Historical Background on Labanotation Textbooks

The authoritative textbook *Labanotation - The System of Analyzing and Recording Movement*, was first published in 1954. The revised and expanded version, published in 1970 (reprinted in 1977) drew attention to a number of topics which were to be dealt with in greater detail in a subsequent publication, referred to as "Part Two". The need for such statements was high-lighted by the reaction of a group in Japan, who, when studying the 1954 Labanotation textbook assumed that it presented the whole system. Since no handling of long sleeves was included, they decided that the system did not meet their needs. It was therefore important to make clear that much more existed. Labanotation did indeed have the capacity of meeting their needs, and in a wider context it was necessary to draw attention to the fact that the system was applicable across the whole spectrum of human movement.

Detailed information on advanced Labanotation usage has not been generally available. Three volumes on advanced topics were published in 1991 and the present series continues the detailed and more advanced material along the same lines.

Labanotation and *Kinetography Laban, Motif Description* and *Structured Description*

The above terms may need some clarification. The specific subject of this book is *Labanotation*, the name given in the United States to the system of movement notation originated by Rudolf Laban and first published in 1928. Most European notators and dance scholars refer to the system as *Kinetography Laban*. There are some differences between Labanotation and Kinetography in notation usages, and occasionally in symbols and rules, and since 1959 the International Council of Kinetography Laban (ICKL) has provided a successful platform for discussions between practitioners on unification and further applications of the system. Differences are now small so that mutual understanding of scores is ensured. Kinetography rules and usages are catalogued in Albrecht Knust's 1979 Dictionary (see Bibliography).

The aim of the present series of texts is to provide a guide to the *Structured Description* of movement, the fully-fledged notation offering a determinate description of the movement progression by detailing choreographed (or otherwise set) actions. A different and complementary approach is provided by *Motif Description (Motif Writing)*, which uses symbols to represent movement ideas and concepts and provide a general statement concerning the theme or motivation of a movement.

The term Labanotation is used in this book to refer to the notation system in general and not to mark an opposition with Kinetography or Motif Writing.

Source materials

Advanced Labanotation contains, whenever possible, systematic discussion of other usages and, where appropriate, comments on the history of symbols and rules and the reason for their inclusion in the Labanotation system. The material presented is based on all available textbooks, on earlier writings of Knust and Maria Szentpál, as well as on personal discussions and correspondence with specialists such as Sigurd Leeder, Valerie Preston-Dunlop and members of the Dance Notation Bureau in New York and the Dance Notation Bureau Extension at Ohio State University. Another major source of information are the proceedings of twenty ICKL Conferences.

Much use is made of the comprehensive theoretical account of the system by Knust, summarized in his *Dictionary of Kinetography Laban/Labanotation* (1979), and his earlier publications including his eight-volume encyclopedia of 1946-50 entitled *Handbuch der Kinetographie Laban*. The textbook *Dance Notation. Kinetography Laban* by Szentpál, published in Hungarian between 1969 and 1976, is unfortunately not readily accessible to readers outside Hungary, but Szentpál generously provided an English translation for her many colleagues.

In many cases, writing an advanced text of this kind has meant breaking new ground: the intricacies of writing sequential movements, successions, and body waves, for instance, were not adequately covered, and some not included at all, in the 1979 Knust Dictionary. Some recent developments in the system such as 'DBP' (Direction in relation to the location of Body Part), track pins and symbols for 'design drawing' came too late to be included in Knust's 1979 Dictionary.

The Advanced Labanotation series offers the latest research on the Labanotation system and hence is completely up-to-date as at the date of publication.

Research Involved

A major concern in the research for this book has been the comparison of one rule against another to check applicability in all contexts. Often this has led to discoveries producing new arguments for or against a certain way of writing.

Labanotation is rapidly developing and is accepted as a tool in recording, research and in education. Each of these fields has specific requirements. There is a call for maximum flexibility in the notation system, so that it can provide general and simple statements for particular purposes and at the same time be very precise where such specificity is required. In dance research the need for precision has increased to the point where we are obliged to consider questions about the system that only ten years ago did not seem important, let alone when the fundamentals of the system were devised. In this new text we have tried to take these different needs into account while respecting the system as it has been handed down to us and is now used by people all over the world.

Notes

These annotations are mainly of three kinds. Firstly, they identify all other major *rules and usages*. Secondly, they mark symbols and rules that have been *recently introduced* or *not described in other sources*. And, finally, they give the sources of certain notation excerpts.

On important or controversial issues, a short discussion of rationale is included. Sometimes, old ways of writing are briefly mentioned.

Research of other usages systematically involved *Táncjelírás, Laban Kinetográfia* by Szentpál and the *Dictionary of Kinetography Laban (Labanotation)* by Knust (see Bibliography, p.72). Where needed, other sources were also used.

Numbers in parentheses at the end of each note indicate where the note is in the text. The following abbreviations identify sources, for full bibliographic information see Bibliography.

References

H36-39	Hutchinson 1936-39 notes
H70	Hutchinson 1970
H83	Hutchinson 1983
ICKL	International Council of Kinetography Laban
K79	Knust 1979
LNTR	*The Labanotator*
AHG	Ann Hutchinson Guest.

1   See H70: 710 and K79: 355b. (1.2)

2   In this analogy with a caterpillar the head end is taken to be the 'free end' just as humans consider the head to be the 'free end'. Another analogy can be made with a hose pipe with which one can produce a ripple from the base where it is being held to the extremity, the free end. (1.7)

3   Sigurd Leeder contributed the V signs ca. 1936. The outflowing signs and the double body wave signs are used in technique studies notated 1936-9. See also H36-39. The sign was officially adopted at the 1967 ICKL conference. (2.1)

4   When drawn on the Labanotation program, *Calaban*, the default sign for
sequential movement is slightly narrower than that established for these signs.
The signs of **2a** and **2b** on page 7 have been adjusted. (2.1)
          Sign as drawn by *Calaban*: ∨
        Sign as it occurs in this book: ∨

5   The drawings of **2c** and **2d**, found in some textbooks, e.g. K79: 355c and d,
are incorrect because they are too long and relate visually to the 'toward' and
'away' signs. (2.1)

6   Such 'unfolding', a commonly used term, is not to be confused with the
unfolding sign used as a cancellation for a previous indication of folding. (3.1)

7   It has also been common practice to write the appropriate pin
followed by a duration line to give the duration, as in the example
given here. Because this pin is not placed within the vertical
'passing state' bow, the *spatial displacement will remain* at the
end of the movement. This description states two facts: a
displacement and a succession; it should only be used when it is
the intention *not to return to the original alignment*. (4.3)

8   The terms 'leading' and 'guiding' have specific applications (see H83,
p.158). A joint *leads* by moving ahead (bulging out) at the start of the
movement; this leading disappears gradually as the movement draws to its end.
A surface or edge *guides*; the limb adjusts at the start (usually through a slight
rotation) and can continue to lead until the movement ends. (5.1)

9   See H70, pp.414 - 433 for Systems of Reference. Note that the term 'Body
Twisted Part Key' is now more appropriately called 'Individual Body Part
System of Reference'. (9.6)

10   Leeder's awareness of and concern with the origins and terminations for
movements in the limbs and torso was more highly developed than in other
similar forms of dance techniques. This led him to evolve a simple method of
indicating these differences, in particular for the arms. First developed ca. 1937
at Dartington Hall, England, this usage has been adopted as a practical
convention. It was first published in *Dance Notation Record*, Vol. II, No. 3,
September 1944. (10.1)

11   An important feature of the Jooss-Leeder style of dance and in the Central
European modern dance training, based on Laban's teachings, was the contrast

between *central* and *peripheral* movement. They were an important part of the study of Eukinetics, which investigated the quality and dynamics in movement. Here we are concerned with *physically* central movement in contrast to *spatially* central. The point in the body from which a movement is initiated was important as well as to what extent the central parts of the body (in particular the parts of the torso) were involved in movements of the arms and legs. Sigurd Leeder sought to express these differences in notation. He showed a definite initiation from the shoulder area by adding a dot within the V sign. The origin of this dot was from the place middle sign, the 'base' point for the limb (arm or leg). This dot was written quite small, not to be confused with approaching the focal point. As a rule the approaching (toward) sign is written longer than the small V for sequential movement. Similarly, use of a small x within the V sign is not confused with approaching a state of flexion because the latter must be shown with a narrower or longer V sign. (11.1)

12   "The shoulder = a thermometer of passion (the word passion here signifies impulse, excitement, vehemence)." (Stebbins 1977, p.18)
"The shoulder intervenes in all forms of emotion." (Stebbins 1977, p.123)
"Delsarte called the three joints (shoulder, elbow and wrist)
the'thermometers'..... The shoulder he called the Thermometer of Passion (here meaning any strong emotion.)" (Shawn 1954, p.41) (11.2)

13   The indication for a central sequential movement is distinctive from the sign for approaching a focal point, both in the shape of the v and the size of the dot. In i) the v has more of a right angle and the dot is small. The v of ii) is narrower, starting at a sharper point and the dot is drawn as a black circle. Once timing needs to be shown the difference is even more evident as can be seen from iii) and iv). (11.3)

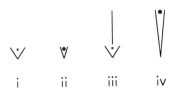

  i   ii   iii   iv

14   Laban dropped the aspects of central and peripheral when he developed his Effort analysis. For industrial and other general movement needs he replaced them with direct and indirect (flexible), the path or shape of the movement. There are no Effort/Shape symbols for central or peripheral. While admiring Laban's Effort development, Jooss regretted this omission seeing awareness and use of central and peripheral as being very much part of expressive dance. He

pointed out that we need the distinction between spatially central and peripheral and physically central and peripheral. Both of these are included in the set of Dynamic signs developed by AHG, published in LNTR No. 40, April 1985. (11.4)

15   A deeper central movement, drawn as **v)**, is distinguished from 'becoming narrower', **vi)**, by the shape of the v. The difference is particularly clear when duration needs to be shown as in **vii)** and **viii)**. (11.5)

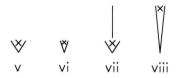

v   vi   vii   viii

16   Body Waves were published in *Dance Notation Record*, Vol. III, No. 1, March 1945. (15.1)

17   The meaning of the Time Signs will be discussed fully in a separate issue of <u>Advanced Labanotation</u>. (16.1)

18   Theoretically, the possibilities described for outward sequences and successions are also applicable to inward sequences, however, other than for the arms these are physically much harder to do, rarely met and hence only a few are being explored here. (17.1)

19   Body Popping is the name given to a form of Street Dancing in which isolated body parts are moved in a sudden accepted way. (17.1)

20   From *Water Study* by Doris Humphrey (1927), notated by Odette Blum, The Dance Notation Bureau, 1971, p.9. Courtesy of Charles Woodford. (17.3)

21   Dynamic Signs will be discussed in the <u>Advanced Labanotation</u> issue on dynamics. (18.1)

22   Ex. **18f** notated by Susie Watts Margolin, 1972. Courtesy of Charles Woodford. (18.5)

23   Ex. **18g** see note 22. (18.6)

24   Ex. **18h** is taken from *Fundamental Training Exercises*. Choreography by Ted Shawn, notated by Jennifer Scanlon, checked and completed by AHG,

1983, p.17. Courtesy of The Language of Dance® Centre. (18.7)

25 Ex. **18i** see note 22. (18.8)

26 From *Incense* by St. Denis. Courtesy of Karoun Tootikian. (18.9)

27 *Lovely Hula Hands*, traditional Hawaiian dance, notated by AHG in the early 1950s. (18.10)

28 Exs. **18m**, **n**, **o**, and **p** are modified from notation of Jooss-Leeder technique by AHG in 1966. Courtesy of The Language of Dance® Centre. (18.12)

29 As taught by Marcia Heard. First notated by Veronica Dittman, January 1998, and subsequently checked for performance detail by AHG with Marcia Heard, June 1998. (18.14)

30 This position of the hand is sometimes described as a contraction of the palm, the result is the same. (18.14)

31 Use is made here of the 8/8 scale, 1/6 contraction on the 6/6 scale being too little, 2/6 being too much. (18.14)

32 Ex. **18q** and **18r** are taken from *Fundamental Training Exercises* (see note 24), p.19. (18.16)

33 Exs. **18s**, **t**, and **u** are from *Water Study* (see note 20), pp.vi and 17. Courtesy of Charles Woodford. (18.18)

34 Before the Time Signs were introduced a change of speed within one movement was indicated by two different lengths of the same direction symbol tied with a bow. A shorter symbol followed by a longer one indicated a slowing down of the movement within the allotted span of time; the reverse described a speeding up. The Time Sign for change of speed can be placed within the symbol or next to it in an addition bracket. (18.19)

Bibliography

Dance Notation Record, bulletin, vols. i-xi, Dance Notation Bureau, New York, 1943-1960.

Hutchinson, Ann. Notebooks from Jan. 1936-July 1938, while at the Jooss-Leeder Dance School.

Hutchinson, Ann. *Labanotation, The System of Analyzing and Recording Movement*, Theatre Arts Books, New York, 1970. (1st published 1954; revised 3rd edition published in 1977).

Hutchinson Guest, Ann. *Your Move, A New Approach to the Study of Movement and Dance*, Gordon and Breach, London, 1983 (3rd reprinting with corrections in 1995).

Hutchinson Guest, Ann. *A History of the Development of the Laban Notation System*, Cervera Press, London, 1995.

Knust, Albrecht. *A Dictionary of Kinetography Laban (Labanotation)* (2 vols.), MacDonald and Evans, Plymouth, England, 1979.

The Labanotator, bulletin, issues 1-25 published 1957-65 by the Dance Notation Bureau, New York; issues 26-77 published 1978-1994 by the Language of Dance® Centre, London.

Proceedings of the Biennial Conferences of the International Council of Kinetography Laban (ICKL), 1959-1999.

Shawn, Ted. *Every Little Movement*, M. Witmark and Sons, 1954.

Stebbins, Genevieve. *Delsarte System of Expression*, Dance Horizons, New York, 1977.

Szentpál, Maria. *Táncjelírás. Laban-Kinetográfia* (Dance Notation. Kinetography Laban). Népmüvelési Propaganda Iroda, Budapest, 1969-76 (3 vol., vol.I 2nd. ed., 1st ed. 1964).

Index

1.3, 5.2 etc. refer to paragraph numbers
1e, 6a etc. refer to example numbers
*S*1, *S*2 etc. refer to section numbers
*n*1, *n*2 etc. refer to end note numbers
p.1, p.2 etc. refer to page numbers

\- replaces the entry word(s)

In the longer listings, the more relevant references are placed first, separated from the others by a semi-colon (;).

accent, strong, 16.1
accompanying arm movements, 18.2-4
Advanced Labanotation Series, p.xi, App.,
  *n*17, *n*21
alignment
- normal -, 7.4, 12.3, 13.3, 15.3
- return to -, 4.1, 5.3, 5.5, 15.4, 18.14, *n*7
analysis
- of sequential movement, *S*1
- of succession in torso, 13.2
- Effort -, *n*14
appearance, 4.6, 5.5
approaching the focal point (*see* also
  'toward' sign), *n*11, *n*13
arabesque, 3.2
arched backward, chest, 16.2, 18.18
arm
- , accompanying - movements, 18.2-4
- , central sequences/successions, 11.1-5
- circle, 18.2-4, 18.6-7, 18.18
- , edges of, 5.1
- , exclusion of, 9.2, 10.6
- , inner surface of, 4.4, 5.4
- , lower, 4.1, 8.2, 14.5
- , outer surface of, 5.2
- , partial sequences/successions, *S*10
- , parts of, 4.7, 14.5, 14.7
- , passive reaction, 8.2, 9.2
- , rotary actions within, *S*8
- , rotation of, 4.4, 5.4, 7.1-2, *S*8, **9o**,
  10.5, 14.7, **18e, 18p**
- , sequential movements in, **4a**, 6.1-3,
  7.1-2, *S*10, 11.1-5, 14.5-7, 18.2-4,
  18.11-12, 18.14
- sliding, 18.7-8
- , spatially closed position, 14.5
- , stretched, 14.5
- successions, *S*4, *S*5, 6.4, **17a**
- - with rotations, *S*8
- swings, 18.8, 18.16
- , upper, 4.1, 7.1, 14.5

articulation
- at waist, 13.3
- , degree of, 15.3
- in base joint of fingers, 9.7
- in wrist joint, 9.4, 9.7
- , limb, 5.1
- no - in hand, 10.3, 18.11
- pelvis -, 15.12
- spinal -, 15.12
Asian Pacific dance, p.xiii, 5.1, 8.1, 9.6
Atlas (vertebrae), 13.2
augmented
- chest, 17.4
- chest tilt, 18.7
- spatially, 15.1
'away', sign for, *n*5

backward
- , arms sliding, 18.8
- body wave, **15e, 15r-s, 18c**
- circle of arms, 18.6
- displacement, 4.4
- sequential leg gesture, 3.3, p.9
- , unfolding, 18.6
balance
- , off, 18.17
- , counter, 15.7, 18.7
base, 1.5, 1.7-8, 2.2, 7.2
- , flow out from - of limb, 10.2
- of chest, 11.4
- knuckles/joint of fingers, 9.7, 10.4,
  18.14
- of spine/torso, 1.6, 12.1, 13.3, 14.1-2,
  15.1
bending of torso (*see* also folding,
  contracting), 18.8, 18.17
bent, neither-stretched-nor-, 14.2
body
- , elongated, 15.9
- , extremity of, 17.7
- , involvement of, 15.1, 15.10

body (cont.)
- , normal alignment, 15.3
- popping, *n*19
- , successive inclusion of, 17.6
- Key, 13.4
- System of Reference for Individual Part, 9.6, *n*9
body wave, *S*15; p.xiii, *S*16, 17.8, 18.2-4, 18.16-19, p.63, *n*3
- , backward, **15e, 15r-s, 18c**
- , circle/circular, 18.2-3, *n*16
- , diagonal forward left, **15g, 15o-p**
- , direction of, 15.3
- , forward, 15.4; **15b, 15h-l, 15q, 17l, 18a**, 18.16
- in different directions, 15.6-7
- in more than one direction, 15.8
- indicating - action, 15.11
- , sagittal, 18.2
- , sign, 15.2, *n*3
- , slow, 15.1, 16.2
- with accompanying arm movements, 18.2-4
bow, 4.6, 5.4
- , deviation, 5.4
- , exclusion, **9e**
- , inclusion, 17.5
- , passing state, 2.3, *n*7
- , vertical, 2.3, 4.3, 5.3, 11.2, 12.3, *n*7
bracket
- , addition, *n*34
- , vertical, 15.11

Calaban, p.v, p.xv, *n*4
cancellation, 4.7, *n*6
caterpillar, 1.7, 1.10, *n*2
center
- of staff, 10.2, 10.5
- of torso, 11.1, 11.4-5
- line, elimination of, 15.3
- of weight, shift of, 18.5
centered fall, 18.7
central
- initiation, 11.1, 11.3, 11.5, **18n**
- involvement, 11.3
- outpouring, 11.4
- rotation, 8.1
- (sequential) movement, *S*11; 18.12
changing speed (*see also* slowing down), *n*34
chest, 7.3-4, 11.3, 13.3, 15.4, 17.3-5
- arched (folded) backward, 16.2, 18.18
- , augmented, 17.4
- augmented - tilt, 18.7
- , movement originating at base of, 11.4
- , knees-to-, 18.6
- leading, 18.5
- shift, 17.1
- -to-waist, 18.5
- , waist-to-, 17.5
circle/circling (*see* also circular)
- arms, 18.2-4, 18.6-7, 18.18

- body wave, 18.2-3, *n*16
- head, 17.4-5
- , lateral, 18.3
- , sagittal, 15.5
- , sequential, 15.4
- , shoulder, 18.14
- , somersault, 15.5
circular (*see* also circle)
- body wave, 15.7, 15.9, *n*16 (*see* also body wave)
- design/pattern/path, 15.1, 15.5, 17.4
- path sign, 17.5
closed position, spatially, 14.5
collapse, 18.17
column, use of adjacent, 6.3
contracted/contracting
- position, 18.16, 18.18
- , sequential movements for, *S*14
- the torso, 14.1, 18.16
counter balance, 15.7, 18.7
cranium, inclusion of, 13.2
curved bow, 2.3, 4.3, 4.6
curving the spine, 14.1

Dance Notation Bureau, New York, p.63, *n*20
Dartington Hall, England, *n*10
decrease signs, 2.1
degree
- of articulation, 15.3
- of displacement, 13.5
- of preparation, 15.3
- of rotation, 4.4, 8.3, 14.7
Delsarte System of Expression, *n*12
Delsarte, François, 11.2, *n*12
design, circular, 15.1
detailed notation, 11.4, 15.1, 15.11, 18.18
deviation, 5.2
- , direction of, 13.4
- , double, 5.6
- bow, 5.4
- downward, 5.5
- upward, 4.6-7, **5a, b, d, h, i, k**
diamond representing space, 13.5
Dictionary of Kinetography Laban, p.62, p.67
diminishing speed, 16.1
direct, *n*14
direction
- , body waves in different, 15.6-7
- , body waves stressing more than one, 15.8
- , change of, p.xiii, 1.5-9, 2.2-3, 12.1, 13.1-2
- of body wave, 15.3
- of deviation, 13.4
- of displacement, 4.2-4, 4.6, 9.5-6; **5a-b, d-g, i-k, 6f, 8i-k, 9g-h, 10g, j, p, 13c-f, k-n, 18q**
- of main thrust, 15.3
- , reverse/reversing, 7.4, 17.8
- , Standard, 13.4
- symbol/sign, 2.3

displacement, 4.2-4, 4.6-7, 9.5-6; **5a-b, d-g, i-k, 6f, 8i-k, 9g-h, 10g, j, p, 13c-f, k-n, 18q,** *n*7
- , appearance and subsidence, 4.5-7, 5.5
- arm, 4.2-7
- , degree of, 13.5
- hand, 9.5-6
- of body wave, 15.1, 15.3
- pelvis, 13.3
- shoulder, 4.1, 11.2
- , size of, 13.5; p.xiii, 15.1, 15.3
- , two, 4.3
double
- body wave sign, *n*3
- deviation, 5.6
- part leading, 5.6
Duncan, Isadora, 15.1
duration, 15.2, *n*15
- , shorter, 2.4
- line, 2.2, *n*7
dynamics (coloring/qualities), 18.1, 18.5, 18.16-17, *n*11, *n*14, *n*21

edge
- , little finger-, 5.5
- of arm, 5.1
- , thumb-, 5.2, 5.4, **8e**, 9.7
education, p.64
Effort
- analysis, *n*14
- sign, 18.18
elbow, 1.3, 4.1, *n*12
- contraction, 18.14
- , flowing through, 1.3, 4.1
- , leading of, 10.2, 18.3
- moving last, 14.6
- rotation, 8.1-4
- , starting from, 10.5, 18.11
- , terminating at, 10.2, 18.11
elongated body, 15.9
elongating the spine, 14.2
emotional basis, 11.2, 11.4
emphasis (*see* also stressed)
- , one-sided, 15.10
ending (*see* also termination),
- at elbow, 10.2, 18.11
- at fingers, 10.4
- at hand, 10.4
- at wrist, 10.3, 18.11
- part for a sequence/succession, 10.2-4
energy, 5.5, 15.10
- , (out)burst of, 15.1, 16.1
Eukinetics, *n*11
European modern dance, 15.1, *n*11
Every Little Movement, *n*12
exclusion
- , arm, 9.2
- bow, 9.2
- , hand, 8.2
- , wrist, 9.3
Expression, Delsarte System of, *n*12

expressive/expression, 9.4, 11.3, 14.7, *n*12, *n*14
extremity
- , concluding at, 12.1
- , emanating, escaping through, 15.1
- , initiating/starting at, 1.8, 7.2-3, 12.1, 14.2, 17.7-8

facing
- , palm, 1.3, 4.6, 5.2, 9.5
- , thumb(-edge), 1.3, 5.4
fall, 18.7-8, 18.17
- and recovery, 18.8
- , centered, 18.7
fingers
- , (base) joints of, 9.3, 9.7, 10.4, 18.14
- , tips of - leading, **7n**
- , stopping at, 10.4
finish (*see* ending)
flexed limb, 2.2
flexing, 5.1, 18.14
flexibility of hand, 9.4, 9.7
floor, sequential torso movements on, p.29
'flop', 18.13
flow, 1.2, 2.1
- , inward, 14.3
- , outward, 10.2, 14.3, 15.1, 17.8
- , wave-like, 12.3
focal point, approaching, *n*11, *n*13
focus, 15.10
- of sequential movements, successions, 3.1
- on a part leading, 11.6
folding
- , chest, 16.2
- , elbow, 1.3
- , hand, 18.14
- , sequential movements for, *S*14, 18.6
- , sideward, 18.5
- , torso, 14.3, 15.12, 18.6, 18.8
- , wrist 1.3
Folkwang Hochschule, 15.4
foot
- ,ball of, 18.10
- leading, 3.3, 17.7
- , re-align, 7.4
forward
- body wave, 15.4; 15.8, 15.10, 15.12, 16.2, 17.8, **18a**, 18.16
- sequential leg gesture, 3.1-2
- shift, 13.3, 15.12, 18.6, 18.18
- succession, 13.5
free end, *n*2
front surface, 14.1

general idea/statement/notation, p.63-64, 13.5, 15.2, 15.9, 15.13, 18.18
Graham technique, 7.3
guidance (*see* also leading)
- , surface of limb, *S*5; 4.2
- , thumb edge, 5.2

guidance (cont.)
-       , timing of, 5.3

half-toe, starting on, 15.9
hand, 4.1, 7.1
-       displacement, 9.5
-       , exclusion of, 8.2
-       flexibility, 9.4, 9.7
hand (cont.)
-       involvement, 9.1
-       , folding of, 18.14
-       moves first, 14.6
-       , no articulation, 10.3
-       , passive/neutral, 10.3
-       ripple, *S*9, 18.9-10
-       succession, 8.5, *S*9, 18.10, 18.14
-       , terminating in, 10.4
-       , weight on, 18.8
head
-       circle/circular pattern, 17.4-5
-       involvement, 13.2
-       leading, 7.5, 12.3
-       , passive, 13.3, 14.4, 15.4, 18.15
-       pelvis-to-, 14.4
-       rotation, 17.5
-       shift, 17.1
-       , spiralling path of, 17.6
-       starting at/moves first, 1.9, 17.3-4
-       -to-pelvis, 17.3
head end, *n*2
heaviness/heavy, 18.16-17
heels, raising of, 15.9
hip
-       jutting out, 13.3
-       leading,. 11.6
-       lifting, 18.10
-       , starting from, 11.6
-       sway, 18.10
history of symbols, p.63
horizontal staple, 6.3
Humphrey, Doris, 17.3, 18.5-6, 18.8, 18.18
Hutchinson (AHG), p.67, *n*3, *n*14, *n*24,
        *n*27-29

ice skating, 7.4
ICKL (*see* International Council of
        Kinetography Laban)
impulse, *S*16; 15.1
-       , spatially large, 16.1
Incense, 18.9
inclusion (*see* also involvement)
-       bow, 17.5
-       , successive, 17.6
increase
-       in speed, 18.17, *n*34
-       in use of parts of torso, 17.4
-       signs, 2.1, 15.2
indirect (flexible), *n*14
individual interpretation, 16.3
initiation (*see* also origin, source and start),
        p.xiii, 15.10
-       , central, *S*11

-       from the extremity, 7.2
-       , shoulder (area), 4.1, 11.1-2
inner source, 15.1
inner surface
-       , arm, 4.4, 5.4
-       , thigh, 3.2
-       , lower leg, 3.2
International Council of Kinetography Laban
        (ICKL), p.62-63, *n*3
interpretation, individual, 16.3
inverted sequence, 7.4
involvement
-       , central, 11.3-6, **18n**
-       , cranium, 13.2
-       , head, 13.2
-       , lower torso, 11.6
-       , shoulder (area), 11.1, 11.3, 18.11-12
-       , whole body, 15.1
inward
-       flow, 1.8, 14.3, 17.1
-       rotation/twist, 4.4, 5.4, 7.1, 8.3, 18.4,
        18.14
-       sequential movement, 1.8-9, *S*17; 7.2,
        12.3, 15.1, *n*18
-       succession, 1.10, 17.1; 3.3, 7.2
-       turn, 7.1

joints of the fingers, 9.3
-       base, 9.7
Jooss, Kurt, p.65, *n*14
Jooss-Leeder, p.xv, 11.1, 15.4, 18.2,
        18.12-13, 18.15, *n*11, *n*28
jump/spring, 18.8, 18.16

Key (*see* System of Reference)
Kinetography Laban, p.62-63, p.67
knees-to-chest, 18.6
knuckles, 9.3, 10.4, 18.14
Knust, Albrecht, p.62-63, p.67

Laban, Rudolf, p.62, *n*11, *n*14
Labanotation, Advanced Series, p.xi, App.,
        *n*17, *n*21
large, spatially, 13.5, 16.1, 18.15
lateral circle, 18.3
leading
-       , chest, 18.5, 18.8
-       , elbow, 10.2, 18.3
-       , feet, 17.7
-       focus on - part, 11.6
-       , head, 7.5, 12.3
-       , hip, 11.6
-       , little finger-edge, 5.5, 9.7
-       , pelvis, 7.5
-       , shoulders, 1.2, 11.2
-       , surface, *S*5; 9.7
-       , sternum, 18.8
-       , thumb-edge, 5.5, 9.7
-       , upper arm, 7.1
Leeder
-       , Jooss-, p.xv, 11.1, 15.4, 18.2,
        18.12-13, 18.15, *n*11, *n*28

Leeder (cont.)
- , Sigurd, p.xv, 10.1, p.63, *n*3, *n*10, *n*11
leg
- gesture, *S*3; 11.6
- , sequential movement of, *S*3, 11.6, 18.13
- , stretching, 15.9
lift
- of weight, 7.4
- base of spine, 12.1
light, 18.18
limb, p.xiii
- articulations, 5.1
- , bent/flexed, 1.7, 2.2
- surface, *S*5; 4.2, 4.4
limited sequential movement/succession, 9.2, 10.2
limp (*see* relaxed)
line
- , duration, 2.2, *n*7, *n*13, *n*15
- , elimination of center, 15.3
little finger-edge, 5.5, 9.7
lower
- arm, 4.1, 4.7, 7.1, 8.2, 14.5
- leg, 3.2-3
- torso involvement, 11.6
lying down from sitting, 1.6, 12.1
lying prone, 17.3

manner of performance, 12.1, 13.3, 14.5, 15.12
measurement sign, 13.5, 18.15
modern dance, European, 15.1, *n*11
Motif Writing, p.62-63
movement (*see* also sequential movement)
- , central, *S*11; 18.12, *n*14
- concepts, p.63
- ideas, p.63
- in opposition, 18.2, 18.4
- motivation, p.63
- origin of, 10.5-6, 11.4-5, *n*10
- , peripheral, *n*11, *n*14
- , preparatory, 15.2, 16.1
- progression, p.62
- , snake-like, 17.1-2
- , sustained, 16.1
- theme, p.63

narrow (*see* also small), 18.6, *n*4, *n*11, *n*13, *n*15
neck, 13.3
neutral hand, 10.3
normal (alignment), return to, 2.2, 4.1, 4.3, 7.1, 11.2, 12.3, 13.3, 15.3-4
- extension, 18.10
notation
- detailed, 11.4, 15.1, 15.11, 18.18
- general (*see* general idea / statement / notation)

off balance, 18.17
one-sided emphasis, 15.10

opposition, move in, 18.2, 18.4
origin of a sequence or succession (*see* also initiation, source, start), 10.5-6, 11.4-5, *n*10
outer
- edge/side of V sign, 10.2
- surface of arm, 5.2
outflowing sign, *n*3
outward
- flow, 1.3, 10.2, 10.5, 14.3, 15.1, 17.8
- , origin of - sequence or succession, 10.5-6, 11.4-5, *n*10
- rotation, 3.2, 4.4, 7.1, 7.2, 8.1-2, 8.4, 18.14
- sequential movement, 1.5-6, *S*3, **4a**, *S*10, *S*11, 14.3, 14.7, 15.1, **18a-i, l-o**
- spiral, 17.6
- succession, 1.7, 7.2, **10g, j, m, p, 11c**, 13.1, 13.3, **18j-k, p-q**
- turn, 7.1
overcurve step, 18.10
overlapping sequences/successions, *S*6, 17.2, 18.12

palm
- facing, 1.3, 4.6, 5.2, 9.5
- sliding, 17.3
part(s) leading, 1.2
- , double, 5.6
- , focus on, 11.6
partial sequence, *S*10; 18.11-12
parts
- of arm, 4.7, 14.5, 14.7
- of torso, 14.1-2, 17.4, 17.7, *n*11
passing state bow, 2.3, *n*7
passion, thermometer of, 11.2, *n*12
passive
- arm, 8.2, 9.2
- hand, 10.3
- head, 13.3, 14.4, 15.4, 18.15
path
- , circular, 15.5, 17.5
- , of pelvis, 15.5, 15.7
- , spiralling, 17.6
pelvis, 7.3-5, 15.1, 15.4-7, 15.10, 17.2
- displacement of, 13.3
- , head-to-, 17.3
- , leading with, 7.5
- , path of, 15.5, 15.7
- preparatory movement, 16.1
- shift, 13.3, 15.7, 18.18
- -to-head, 7.3, 14.4
performance, manner of, 1.1, 2.1, 4.2, 12.1, 13.3, 14.5, 15.12
physically
- central movement, *n*11, *n*14
- peripheral movement, *n*11, *n*14
pin, 4.3, 9.5, 13.3, *n*7
pivot turn, sequential, 7.4-5
placement, normal, 4.3
plié, deep, 15.4, 15.9, 18.6
preparation, 3.2, 15.3, 15.6-7

preparation (cont.)
- , degree of, 15.3
preparatory
- movements, 15.2, 16.1
- jump, 18.16
presign, 2.3
pressure, 18.5
Preston-Dunlop, Valerie, p.63
previous alignment/state, return to, 2.2, 5.3

raising the heels, 15.9
reaching up, 18.16
Reading Examples, S17, S18
recovery, fall and, 18.8
relaxation/relaxed, 18.5, 18.13, 18.17
research, p.63-64, p.67
retiré position, 3.2
return
- to alignment, 5.3, 5.5, 12.3, 15.4, *n7*
- to normal, 2.2, 4.1, 4.3, 7.1, 11.2, 12.3, 15.4, 18.14
- to previous state, 2.2, 5.3
- to upright, 12.2, 15.12, 17.2
reverse/reversing direction, 7.4, 17.8
ripple, p.xiii, 1.10, 5.1, 6.4, 13.3, *n2*
- , hand, S9, 18.9-10
- , speed of, 9.4
rising at end, 15.9
rotation (*see also* rotational), p.xiii
- , arm, 4.4, 5.4, 7.1-2, *S8*, **9o**, 10.5, 14.7, **18e, 18p**
- , arm successions with -, S8
- , degree of, 4.4, 8.3, 14.7
- , elbow, 8.1, 8.3-4
- , inward, 4.4, 8.3, 18.4, 18.14
- , leg, 3.2
- , outward, 3.2, 4.4, 8.2, 8.4, 18.14
- of arm, 4.4, 5.4, 7.2
- of elbow, 8.4
- of leg, 3.2
- , sequential, S7
- within arm, S8

sagittal body wave, 18.2
scarf, 1.5, 1.8
sequential
- actions, adding, 15.12
- circle, 15.4
- contracting, S14
- displacement, 4.4
- folding, S14, 18.6
- gestures, expressive, 9.4
- pivot turns, 7.4
- rotation, S7
- twists, 7.3
- unfolding, 14.4, 18.3
sequential movement/sequence, p.xiii, p.xv, p.63
- , analysis of, S1
- , backward, 3.3, 18.8, 18.18
- , central, S11; 18.12
- , complete, 6.1

- , focus of, 3.1
- , inverted, 7.4
- , inward, 1.8-9, S17; 7.2, 12.3, 15.1
- , method of writing, S2
- of arm, **4a**, 6.1-3, 7.1-2, S10, 11.1-5, 14.5-7, 18.2-4, 18.11-12, 18.14
- of hand, 18.9-10, 18.14
- of leg, S3, 11.6, 18.13
- of torso, S12; 1.6, 1.9, 7.3, 14.1-4, 17.2, 17.7, 18.6, 18.8, 18.15, 18.19
- , origin/source of, 10.5-6, S11, *n10*
- , outward,, 1.5-6, S3, **4a**, S10, S11, 14.3, 14.7, 15.1, **18a-i, l-o**
- , overlapping, S6, 17.2, 18.12
- , partial, S10; 18.11-12
- , separate, 6.1, 9.1, 15.13
- , sideward, 6.1-2, 18.5, 18.10, 18.19
- , sign for, p.7, *n3*; 10.2-5, 11.2-3, 11.5-6, *n3-5, n10-11, n13, n15*
- through spine, 12.2, 15.1, 17.2
Shawn, Ted, 18.7, 18.16-17, *n12*
shift
- , forward, 13.3, 18.6, 18.18
- of center of weight, 18.5
- of chest, 17.1
- of head, 17.1
- of pelvis, 13.3, 15.7, 18.18
shoulder, 11.2, 15.4, 17.1, 17.3-4, 17.7, *n12*
- circle, 18.14
- displacement, 11.2
- , excluded, 8.1
- initiation/starting in, 4.1, 10.2, 11.1
- , involvement of, 1.2, 4.7, 11.1, 11.3, 18.11-12
- leading, 1.2, 11.2
- line, 7.3, 14.1, 14.3
- return to normal, 11.2
- section, 17.7
sideward
- fold, 18.5
- sequential movement, 6.1-2, 18.5, 18.10, 18.19
sign (*see also* symbol)
- , 'away', *n5*
- , body wave (, double), 15.2, *n3*
- , dynamic, 18.1, *n14, n21*
- , Effort, 18.18, *n14*
- , sequential movement, p.7, *n3*; 10.2-5, 11.2-3, 11.5-6, *n3-5, n10-11, n13, n15*
- , Time, 18.19, *n17, n34*
- , 'toward', *n5, n11*
- , unfolding, *n6*
simple statements, p.64
sitting up from lying, 1.9, 12.1
size of displacement, 13.5; p.xiii, 15.1, 15.3
size of succession, 13.5
skating, ice, 7.4
skull, 13.2-3
sliding
- arms, 18.7-8
- palms, 17.3
slow body wave, 15.1, 16.2

slowing down, 18.19, *n*34
small
- forward succession, 13.5
- hand successions, 9.4
- , spatially, **13i-j**
snake-like movement, 17.1-2
soft leg gestures, 3.2
somersault, 13.3, 15.5
source (*see* also initiation, origin, start)
- at wrist, 10.6
- (for research), p.63, p.67
- , inner, 15.1
- of a sequence, *S*11
space, diamond representing, 13.5
Spanish dance, 9.6
spatial/spatially
- augmented, 15.1
- central, *n*11, *n*14
- closed position, 14.5, 14.7
- displacement, 18.5, *n*7
- (very) large, 13.5, 16.1, 18.15
- pattern, 15.4-5
- peripheral, *n*14
- (very) small, 13.5
speed (*see* also ripples)
- , change of, *n*34
- , diminishing, 16.1
spine/spinal (*see* also torso), p.xiii
- articulation, 15.12
- curving, 14.1
- , lengthening, 14.2
- , lifting base of, 12.1
- , sequential movement through, 12.2, 15.1, 17.2
- undulation, 12.2, 13.1, 17.2
- , upper -/torso, 14.1, 14.3, 17.4
spiral/spiralling
- exercise, 7.3
- , outward, 17.6
- path of head, 17.6
spring (*see* jump)
St. Denis, Ruth, 18.9, *n*26
Standard (*see* also System of Reference, Key)
- Cross, 9.6
- directions/Key, 13.4
staple, horizontal, 6.3
start (*see* also initiation, origin, source)
- at base of torso/spine, 1.6, 12.1, 14.1-2, 15.1
- , sudden, 16.1
- with elbow, 10.1, 10.5, 18.3, 18.11
- with extremity, 1.8-10, 7.3, 12.1, 14.2, 17.5, 17.7-8
- with hand, 14.7
- with head, 7.3, 17.4
- with hip, 11.6
- with legs, 7.4
- with shoulder, 10.2, 11.1
- with thigh, 3.1-2, 18.13
- with upper spine, 14.3
- with wrist, 10.6

state
- , passing - bow, 2.3, *n*7
- , return to previous/normal (*see* return to)
- , rotational, 4.4
Stebbins, Genevieve, *n*12
stop (*see* ending)
Street Dancing, 17.1
stressed, not (*see* also emphasis), 14.7
stretched
- arm, 14.5, 14.7
- neither - -nor-bent, 14.2
- torso, 14.2
stretching the legs, 15.9
strong accent, 16.1
Structured Description, p.62
subsidence/subsiding, 4.5-7; 2.2, 5.3-5, 11.3
succession (*see* also sequential movement, successive), *S*4, p.13, *S*5
- , arm - with rotations, *S*8
- , complete, 6.1
- , focus of, 3.1
- , hand, *S*9; 8.5, 10.6, 18.9-10, 18.14
- , inward, 1.10, 17.1; 3.3, 7.2
- , origin of, 10.5-6, *S*11
- , outward, 1.7, 7.2, **10g, j, m, p, 11c,** 13.1, 13.3, 18.15
- , overlapping, *S*6
- sign, 2.2
- , torso, *S*13, 18.15
successive (*see* also sequential)
- flow, 1.2, 4.7
- inclusion/use of body, 17.5-6
- ripple (*see* ripple)
sudden start, 16.1
surface
- , arm, *S*5; 4.4, **18m-n**
- , inner, 3.2, 4.4, 5.4, **18m-n**
- leading, *S*5; 9.7, **18m-n**
- , limb, *S*5; 4.2, 4.4
- , outer, 5.2, **18m-n**
- , thigh, 3.2
- , torso, 14.1, 15.13
sustained movement, 15.1, 16.1
Swan Lake, 8.1
swing, arm, 18.8, 18.16
swivel turn, 7.4
symbols, history of, p.63
symmetry, 18.4, 18.6
System of Reference, *n*9
- Individual Body Part, 9.6, *n*9
- , Standard, 9.6, 13.4
Szentpàl, Maria, p.63, p.67

termination
- of movement (*see* also partial sequence), 10.2-4
- of vertical bow, 12.3
thermometer of passion, 11.2
thigh, 3.1-3, 18.13
thrust, direction of main, 15.3

thrust (cont.)
- ,forward, 18.17
thumb
- -edge guidance/leading, 5.2, 5.4, 5.5, 9.7
- (-edge) facing, 1.3
tilting
- , chest, 18.7
- , torso - as a unit, 12.1
Time Sign, 18.19, *n*17, *n*34
timing, 2.2-3, 15.3, *n*13, *n*15
- of guidance, p.15
torso, p.xiii
- , base of, 1.6, 7.3, 12.1, 13.3, 14.1-2, 15.1
- , center of, 11.1, 11.4-5
- , contracting/bending, 14.1, **18a, c, j, r, s, u** 18.16
- , counter balancing of, 15.7
- , folding, 14.3, 15.6, 15.12, 18.5-6, 18.8, **18v**
- , general usage of, 13.2
- , increasing use of parts/, involvement of parts, 17.4-5
- , involvement of lower, 11.6
- , lengthening, 14.2
- , normal alignment of, 7.4
- , sequential movements for, *S*12; 1.6, 1.9, 7.3, 14.1-4, 17.2, 17.7, **18f-i, u, v**
- , start at base of, 1.6, 12.1, 14.1-2, 15.1
- , stretched/stretching, 14.2, 18.15, **18u, v**
- , successions in, *S*13, 18.15
- , surface of, 14.1, 15.13
- tilting as a unit, 12.1
- turning as a unit, 7.4
- , twist of, 7.3
- unfolding, 14.4, 15.4, 18.6-7
- upper -/spine, 14.1, 14.3, 17.4
'toward' sign, *n*5, *n*11
turn, 18.19
- , head leading in, 7.5
- , inward, 7.1
- of arm, 7.1-2
- of body as a whole, 7.4
- of torso as a unit, 7.4
- of upper body, 7.3
- , outward, 7.1
- , pivot, 7.4-5; p.xiii
- , swivel, 7.4
twist, p.xiii
- , arm, 7.1-2; 8.1, 10.5
- , torso, 7.3-4

undulating/undulation, p.xiii, 1.7, 4.2, 9.4, 11.1, 18.10
- , spinal, 12.2, 13.2, 17.2
- wave, 12.2
unemphasized/unstressed, 1.6, 18.14
unfolding, *n*6
- , arms, 18.3, 18.7
- , hand, 18.14

- , leg, 3.1-2
- sign, *n*6
- , torso, 14.4, 15.4, 18.6-7
unison action, 14.5, 14.7
unit
- , chest-to-waist, 18.5
- , head-to-pelvis, 17.3
- , pelvis-to-head, 7.3, 14.4
- , waist-to-chest, 17.5
uplift, 18.16
upper
- arm, 4.1, 7.1, 14.5
- body, 7.3, 18.7
- spine/torso, 14.1, 14.3, 17.4
upright, 12.2-3, 13.1, 14.1, 15.9, 15.12
- , return to, 17.2
- stance, 13.1
upward deviation/displacement, 4.6-7, **4e-f**, 5.4, 18.15

vertical
- bow, 2.3, 4.3, 5.3, 11.2, 12.3, *n*7
- bracket, 15.11
vibrating finger action, 17.3

waist, 7.3-4, 13.3, 15.4, 18.15
- , articulation at, 13.3
- , chest-to-, 18.5
- , movement originating at, 11.4-5
- -to-chest, 17.5
Water Study, 17.3, 18.18-19
wave, 4.1, 4.5, 18.7
- , body (*see also* body wave), *S*15; 18.2-4, 18.16-19, *n*3
- -like, 12.3, 18.5, 18.19
- , undulating, 12.2
weight, 18.7-8
- , catching, 18.17
- , center of, 18.5
- , lift of, 7.4
Wigman School, Dresden, 15.4
whole torso (*see* torso)
wrist, 4.1, *n*12
- , articulation in, 9.4, 9.7
- , end/stop at, 10.3, 18.11
- , exclusion of, 9.3, 10.3
- folding, 1.3, 18.14
- , passive, 18.11
- , source/starting from, 10.6

Useful Contact Information

Language of Dance Centre
17 Holland Park
London W11 3TD
United Kingdom
Tel: +44 (0) 20 7229 3780
Fax: +44 (0) 20 7792 1794
email: info@lodc.org
www.lodc.org

Dance Notation Bureau Extension
The Ohio State University
Department of Dance
1813 N. High Street
Columbus OH 43210-1307
USA
Tel: +1 614 292 7977
Fax: +1 614 292 0939
web: http://www.dance.ohio-state.edu
e-mail: marion.8@osu.edu

Language of Dance Center
1972 Swan Pointe Drive
Traverse City
MI 49686
USA
Tel: +1 231 995 0998
Fax: +1 231 995 0998
email: Tinalodc@aol.com

The Labanotation Institute
The University of Surrey
Guildford
Surrey GU2 5XH
United Kingdom
Tel: +44 (0)1483 259 351
Fax: +44 (0)1483 300 803
e-mail: J.Johnson-
Jones@Surrey.ac.uk

Dance Notation Bureau
151 West 30th Street, Suite 202
New York NY 10001
USA
Tel: +1 212 564 0985
Fax: +1 212 904 1426
web: http://www.dancenotation.org/
e-mail: notation@mindspring.com

Andy Adamson
Department of Drama and Theatre
Arts
University of Birmingham
P.O. Box 363
Birmingham B15 2TT
United Kingdom
e-mail: a.j.adamson@bham.ac.uk